Other Books by Andrew Keene

The New Wave of Trading:
The Future of Trading Stocks, Options, and Futures
FEBRUARY 2016

Master How to Trade Like a Hedge Fund Manager
FEBRUARY 2016

The World's Best Technical Indicator:
The Ichimoku Cloud
JANUARY 2014

How You Can Make Millions Trading Stocks
and Options Just Like Me
OCTOBER 2013

Keene on the Market:
Trade to Win Using Unusual Options Activity,
Volatility, and Earnings
JULY 2013

Airbnb

A 21st-Century Goldmine

Airbnb

A 21st-Century Goldmine

Andrew Keene
CEO of AlphaShark.com

A POST HILL PRESS BOOK
An Imprint of Post Hill Press

Airbnb
A 21st-Century Goldmine
© 2018 by Andrew Keene
All Rights Reserved

ISBN: 978-1-68261-726-7
ISBN (eBook): 978-1-68261-727-4

Cover Art by Cody Corcoran
Interior Design and Composition by Greg Johnson, Textbook Perfect

Post Hill Press
New York • Nashville
posthillpress.com
Published in the United States of America

Disclaimer

This book is not considered a substitute for financial or investing advice. Its sole purpose is to provide information that will help consumers better understand the Airbnb business model and how it can potentially be a sound investment decision for certain individuals.

Examples within the content of this book are not guarantees of return, or experience.

Andrew Keene, CEO of AlphaShark.com, has no vested interest in Airbnb, and the wisdom that's laid out throughout this book is an accumulation of research, data, and trends from his sound and astute trading strategies, as well as his personal experiences using the Airbnb model, both as a guest and a host.

Acknowledgments

There have been so many people who have literally contributed to helping me and supporting me during this project that I would be remiss if I didn't thank them for all they've done. I appreciate it greatly.

To EO, Entrepreneurship Organization, and to my forum, the fiducies, thank you for the confidence, courage, and understanding of my crazy life throughout the two years we have been together. Without your help, this project would have been considerably more challenging, and I am honored that you accepted me and brought me into your lives. I appreciate it more than words can express. I am equally grateful to Raoul Davis and Leticia Gomex of Ascendant Group Branding for their assistance with certain aspects of this book and for their assistance with my research, always helping to ensure the process kept moving forward.

Without the help and commitment of all the Airbnb owners and hosts, who allowed me to interview them, answered my questions, and willingly gave their time and intellect to make this book the best it could be, I thank you so much. This includes CEO Brian Chesky and Joe Gebbia, who never would have created Airbnb without their dream. And Jill McKellan, thank you for your assistance to polish the abundance of information that was thrown your way.

This is my fifth book and I wish I could thank everyone individually, but I guess that I cannot because I do not have enough space. But, I will save the best for last.

When Ron Arrest won his NBA championship ring playing with the Los Angeles Lakers, he gave his ring to his therapist. He might have gone to more therapy than I did, but thank you Dr. Margaret Sawires for helping me become a better person. Baby Bolt, you might be my little Goldendoodle, but I love you so much. Then there is there is my family. My best and worst brother, Jeffrey Keene, thanks for being the shoulder to cry on when I am sad and strong arms to pick me up when I am down and out. Nancy, Ryan, and my two nephews, I know I am crazy, but thank you for letting be myself and not judging me. Then to my parents, I could never do what I have done in this world without you out. I believe that I inherited the best qualities of each of *you* to make me become the most amazing person I can be, so thanks.

Contents

Foreword

by Vanessa Deleon

I've heard people say that everything in life is either a lesson or blessing. Well, in the case of the author, Andrew Keene, it is a blessing that our paths have crossed, and I'm excited about our future endeavors. I am owner/principal of an interior design firm located in the Chelsea area of Manhattan, Vanessa Deleon Associates, which has been in business for over 15 years. Recently, I have been newly introduced to the Airbnb ecosystem and community. I have designed for some famous residential and commercial sites. Lately, I have been much more involved with clients interested in working on high-end projects for Airbnb, similar to many of the projects involving Andrew. I have watched this ecosystem grow, and I'm thrilled to be a part of this new exciting venture.

I first met Andrew while in Los Angeles auditioning for Andrew's interior designer on primetime TV. Enthralled by his passion, energy, and enthusiasm for Airbnb and building his brand of rentals across the country, I found myself thinking, "Wow, not only does this guy know everything about the Airbnb business model, but he also wants to share his invaluable insight and success to help others." Fortunate enough to sit across from my physical opposite, realizing we may have a lot in common. He is tall, blond, Caucasian male who dresses like a "Cali" boy, while I am a petite brunette with the typical New York style, but we share great synergies and passion for our properties and future.

The expression "a picture is worth a thousand words" reflects our view towards Airbnb properties; every little detail within the property has a significant impact on the result. Andrew's unapologetic directness has motivated and challenged me in ways that I did not think possible. He is frugal about expenses, driven about finding the right Airbnb properties, but I always feel an embracing compassion talking to Andrew not only about business but about any personal problems I may have as well.

The old idiom "you can't judge a book by its cover" does hold true when it comes to Andrew. He looks like one of those California surfer "dudes" who spends his days on the beach, not in a coffee shop working on writing books on how to make money while simultaneously building his brands.

This book is indeed the most impactful and invaluable Airbnb book I have ever read. I loved reading this book filled with insight and wisdom. Andrew breaks it all down, step-by-step in four main sections showing anyone in the United States how they can make money on the Airbnb ecosystem, the process of how to host a property, items a property should have, and how to maximize the revenues of property. He is always willing to help, share, and talk about his expertise on Airbnb, the stock market, and cryptocurrencies.

I highly recommend this book to anyone who is interested in Airbnb as a guest, a host, or someone who is passionate about finance. It could be the step you'll need to true financial freedom.

Introduction

"The starting point of all achievement is desire."

— NAPOLEON HILL —

My life is fast-moving, and has always exposed me to new concepts and ideas. An open mind and a knack for analyzing have led to a lot of amazing opportunities for me.

I would say that this started when I was in high school. Sitting around was never an option for me because I would get easily bored. If I wasn't at the movies, I was driving to Paradise Records to get new release CDs, and then off to work at Super Just Games, where I worked thirty hours a week. We are all wired differently and for me, I just always needed to be busy and constantly learning a new skill or trait.

With this being said, it'll seem strange to you when I mention that by the time I graduated with my finance degree from the University of Illinois at Champaign-Urbana—a top 50 finance school and top 10 business school—I had no damn idea what I was going to do. After all that work I was kind of spinning my wheels as I evaluated everything. So I talked to my go-to source, that is, Dad, about it. He threw out some options.

My dad, what a guy, is a jack-of-all-trades. He was co-general counselor at Ameritech, but as a young kid I always looked up to him because of all the things he was involved in and with. I really did believe that he had the answer for every question I could ask.

So when I didn't know what to do, Dad began to ask me the questions necessary to sort it out.

Did I want to go into being an investment advisor? No.

How about being an analyst? I just couldn't see myself sitting at a desk from 9–5 in a cubicle; I mean come on.

Become a financial advisor? Definitely not.

However, when trading was suggested to me I was immediately interested. I read all the necessary books about trading such as Michael Lewis's *Liar's Poker,* and I was so nervous. I remember as a little kid I once went down to the Chicago Board of Trade and saw all these guys yelling and screaming at each other, and I was like why the @#$% are they wearing yellow jackets as well. I literally thought that they were all nuts and that was not really my style—well, not yet.

Since my parents lived in Deerfield, Illinois, I got a job in a clerk-to-trade program in nearby downtown Chicago with Botta Capital Management. These traders thought they were so good that Botta stood for "Botta Options Traders There Are." Man, I knew I wanted it bad when I was willing to work for two thousand dollars a month, live with my parents for a year-and-a-half, and every morning take the 5:40 train into Chicago to Union Station.

Work started at 6:30 a.m. for me and I knew that in the cutthroat world of trading I was only going to get one chance to prove myself. I will tell anyone who will listen: I did not do any work in college. I went to less than 20 percent of my classes, cheated on so many of my exams, and I was much more into the business of getting my bachelor's in women than I was in finance. Somehow, I still graduated with a 3.4 grade point average and was in a bunch of honor fraternities.

To be honest, I probably had a 3.9 in any math and business class and a 2.5 in the rest.

But now, I was making up for it. I was putting in the time.

I clerked for nine months before finally getting the opportunity to learn to trade. Out of the fourteen who started, only four got to trade. I was going to be one of them. It just seemed to make sense to me. Trading is not about gambling, it's about reward versus risk setup and probability. It is more of game theory, at which I excelled.

Trading is a weird and unique thing. You either get it or you don't. Essentially, you are your own boss making your own money. There's no faking it.

When you trade you have four main choices to focus on: options, stock, forex (foreign exchange currency), or futures. I chose equity options, and that's what I traded for nearly a decade at the pits of the Chicago Board Options Exchange (CBOE). Talk to any trader in New York, tell them that you trade equity options and you get mad respect, because it is the hardest product to trade. There are crazy words like Alpha, Delta, Gamma, Rho, Skew, Theta, and Vega associated with it.

I started in the pit—that insane looking place that you see in movies like *Trading Places*. You get to choose your pit based on one main stock. I started in the GE Pit and traded there for three years. The only reason I traded in that pit was I was told that the traders in the pit were weak. Trading is unlike anything in the world and it all had to do with speed. As you can tell, speed is one of my strongest suits and this is why I knew I could go in that pit and dominate.

My domination plan had a few falters. For over three-and-a-half months, I wanted to go home and cry every night. I still remember it like it was yesterday; there were two traders in the front of the pit who would just stare at me and shake their heads. However, I got to be faster at trading and understand supply and demand curves better, and because of it I finally earned their respect.

From that point on, the experience was incredible and I was making way more money than any of my friends. From my point of view, girls define themselves by how skinny or pretty they are, whereas guys talk about boats, bitches, and watches. Not to brag, but my watch collection is twelve-strong and worth about 100,000 dollars.

My next stop was the Philip Morris Pit, and it was loaded with ups-and-downs there, especially when the State of Illinois sued the company over the supposed deception of indicating light cigarettes were better for you. In the end, Philip Morris won and restructured, and I moved on. I was always long stock in Philip Morris, so I would almost always encourage my friends to smoke (at $10 ten a pack). It was nothing that I would partake in, but I wanted the stock to move higher.

After that I moved into the Apple Pit, which was insane and one of my greatest accomplishments. The only device in the "I-world" we all know today that they had out was the big, clunky, first generation iPod. I was in the trading pit for four years—from 2008 through 2012. I like to tell everyone that I was the largest independent on-the-floor AAPL trader in the world, but the brokerage firms do not like when I say that so I just say "one of the biggest." Not unlike when Mila Kunis said she was "almost eighteen" when she tried out for *That '70s Show*, but was only fourteen, but that's another story.

Most of you look at those years and think about how much the market tanked. But it didn't lose money for everyone. I had my two best trading years in that pit despite the world crumbling and the market toppling and I made over five million dollars trading in those two years. The funny thing is it has always been difficult for me to be long in the stock market after that because I made so much money in a bear market. I will tell anyone who will listen that the stock market is the biggest Ponzi scheme in the world. Why do I say that? If there are more aggressive buyers than sellers of anything—401(k), pension funds, mutual funds—then the price will always go higher.

I was one of the biggest traders in that pit and what really cemented my instincts and skills in the trading arena was that I didn't begin trading until 2003, when most people considered it to be a dying art by that point. When I was a clerk on the trading floor, traders would say that they were going to change the CBOE into a big bowling alley when seat leases were 140,000 dollars. When overturn went up to about 2.5 million dollars, I wished I had a couple of those in my back pocket.

Technology has changed the game for trading, as evidenced by online trading brokerages. Really, everything has changed and it's faster paced and virtual, less face-to-face. The trading floor used to be the first place in the world where brokerage firms would bring their orders; now it's the last. Penny wide options and weekly options killed the business of a market maker, and this is why I have decided to pivot. This makes today's trading the best time ever for retail traders. This is what's exciting about innovative platforms like Airbnb. And it keeps getting crazier.

Conducting business through technology and making money off it is possible if you do your due diligence and operate with urgency.

Today, if you were to look into a pit, you'd see just a handful of traders there, and in the biggest exchange market most of us know—the one on Wall Street—it's more of a television set for CNBC than an actual live, constant action trading floor. I think there is less than 5 percent of traders on the floor than there was ten years ago. There is nothing I would like more than to be on the trading floor like it was 2007 and 2008 again, the best and most fun years of my professional life. The trading floor was like one huge frat house, but with money flying like it was going out of style.

After a decade of successful trading, only having a few poor years, I decided to step away from the dwindling floor and into the expert role. Today, I teach beginner, intermediate, and expert traders about trading and do hits about trading and Airbnb for various business shows on Bloomberg TV, CNBC, and Fox Business. Over the last five years I have done more than five hundred live webinars and taught more than seventy thousand students how to trade. I love teaching, educating, and showing students the real truth about trading. This work suits me. The way it helps connect people with all this great information I've learned via experience and instinct for the market drives me.

People can make a ridiculously large amount of money if they tap into the vein of this type of success. You just have to go for it.

As I grew out of the traditional way of trading and into ways to do this same exciting thing with technology, I got to talking with my then fiancée, Sarah. At this point I had been on CNBC, Bloomberg, and more for almost five years. I never got paid for any of this, but it was fun to text my friends and a group of guys at my gym, East Bank Club. A group of guys called me "Bloomberg," because they did not know my name but would always see me on TV. At my peak, I was filming more than one TV hit a day and was drained from all of it. Sarah mentioned how people were doing wedding blogs and making one hundred thousand dollars, only working twenty hours a week. I was interested and when she asked if she should start one I thought it made sense. It never happened.

Next, as someone who loved to travel, she suggested that we create a travel blog. We were traveling in South America for five weeks, but she hated every picture she was in and could not stay focused on the blog. I was definitely into the entire thing and documenting the adventures we had during our global travels. This was hard, because I never thought I looked good in pictures either, but I did not really care one way or another. Me? I'm just a guy who's thinking, *it's a blog, and no one cares.* Well, almost no one.

On to the next idea.

"How about you do a financial blog?" she asked. That I could do, as it was entirely in my control. That was the birth of my first business, *KeeneOnTheMarket.com.* Year 2012. It was funny, because we would call it KOTM. One day I was looking up KOTM and it stood for Knights of the Maccabees, and I am Jewish, so it was almost fate.

When I began blogging I didn't have a product. It was during the movie about Facebook, *The Social Network,* that I realized that the longer I could go without advertising and revenues, the more I could build a following and the more I could make in the long run. So, I began studying the various business models out there and figured out what I thought was scalable and convertible for me, as well as enjoyable.

Three quick decisions were made:

▶ I don't like teaching people one-on-one about trading. It's tedious and expensive for them. Imagine spending five thousand dollars on training. Are you really going to make more than that? Not with only a twenty-thousand-dollar account.

- ▸ Going into "trading coaching," like a lot of people who left the pit did, was not something I was willing to entertain.
- ▸ Going to work for a brokerage firm as an advisor or to talk with customers about strategies was not in my future.

KeeneOnTheMarket.com was dedicated to teaching people how to trade in a group setting. Over the years, it had trained over seventy thousand students. However, the needs of people shift rapidly and over time, the demand for online classrooms lessened in lieu of a preference for real-time virtual learning experience.

Like I always do, I got back to work researching the trends and best business models. I went through the list of Top 100 financial blogs and wanted to see what others were doing. I wondered how I or anyone else ever had a conversation without Google. Before the internet went mainstream, people would have to debate and discuss topics like, "How much is Mark Cuban's net worth?" Now you can just Google it—3.4 billion dollars. What I found that resonated with me was this guy—I will make him nameless even though I obviously know who he is—who had a business model where people paid to watch him trade. They were paying for his service. Now this I could do.

I paid for his service, went in, and was like *this is a joke, I can do way better than this guy*. Was he a trader from the trading floor? No. To be honest, he did not really know too much. I started to ask around and I heard everyone talk about how much money he made, so this is when I launched our live trading room.

The live trading room launch created a room where we could not get more than sixty people for about a year and a half. Today, we have anywhere from 300-350 people in it on any given day. As the model stands to date, they pay 199 dollars a month and have access to several things, including:

- ▶ Watching five moderators trade with real capital for 7.5 hours daily.
- ▶ Real-time text and email alerts.
- ▶ An active community of traders sharing ideas with each other in real time, where you could stop trading alone.

This has been a great formula. Now I've stepped aside and am online moderating during trade days from when the market opens at 8:30 a.m. (CST) to 9:45 a.m. I will always love the rush of opening bell. Then I pay four other moderators to run the room until the market closes at 3:30 p.m. CST. When I first started working in the trading room I was in there for 4.5 hours of audio daily. Do you know how hard it is to talk to yourself for 4.5 hours a day?

When my brother got married I was his best man and he had the perfect joke. "I love my brother and it's amazing to think he found his passion in life. He gets paid to talk to himself all day." Which is true; anyone who knows me knows I love to talk, and the more I get drunk, the more I love to talk.

People have access to ways to potentially earn a lot of money trading for the price of a Venti® at Starbucks—about eight dollars a day. I know, it sounds like one of those save-the-world statistics. I don't know if it'll save the world, but it will indeed put you on the path to be a better trader. If you want to see some fun and entertainment, I'll give you a forty-nine dollars a month code: alphashark.com/Airbnb

Some people come to the room a little.

Others a lot.

It's completely your choice.

One thing you learn quickly with an online business is that you better have your shit together when it comes to internet marketing. There's a lot to know about what you *should* and *should not* do. I like to tell people that I'm an "internet market genius," self-proclaimed of course. However, how did I learn this? Trial and error and a lot of reading books. I try to read at least thirty books a year. An author puts together what they are an expert on and you can learn it in just a couple of hours. Knowledge is power and power is knowledge, as I say. It's been suggested that a few others have variations of this thought.

People like variety...the "spice of life" or something like that. Because of this, we have ten models for subscriptions. The largest subscription comes from the live trading room and I call it our bread-and-butter product. We have pivoted our company as many times as it was necessary and have sold more than ten thousand courses. But now traders are done with the education and want indicators.

What's an indicator? Indicators are statistics used to measure current conditions as well as to forecast financial or economic trends. These are technical indicators, which together can spit out a buy and sell signal on a chart with stop losses and profit targets—if I want to have my programmer put them on there.

This pivot has been huge, and it is what people want now. We sell about one hundred indicators a month and it's a one-time purchase (currently priced at 299 dollars).

Then there are webinars, which will always remain popular. I've personally hosted five hundred-plus webinars in the past five years. We usually do the same thing at webinars; we teach for forty-five minutes and then we pitch for fifteen minutes.

Many traders come to every single webinar and never buy anything and then other traders come to every webinar and will buy every product. We track all these numbers and they are called Top Tick, at Pitch, and Conversion Rate. The Conversion Rate depends on what the product is, how much it costs, who pitches, and how many other webinars we have done for this so far.

Are you wondering where the hell Airbnb fits into all this? Stick with me.

During all this business growth, I also had a personal life. Granted, it was a bit tumultuous, to put it mildly.

After eight years of togetherness, my fiancée and I broke up. It was bad. Like drinking half a bottle of Scotch and/or vodka for six months in a row bad. This was not simultaneously; it just depended on the night (lol)—sometimes I felt like Scotch and other nights I felt like vodka. However, I had to shake things up and get over it and move on.

I wanted to move to a large city and the weather had to be warm so I visited Dallas, Miami, and San Diego. I made my decision to be California-bound and I chose San Diego. This was the first time I ever used Airbnb to find a place to stay. To be honest, one of my best friends, David Rosenfield, was a big "couch surfer," which I still think is the weirdest concept ever. Airbnb, on the other hand, I figured I would give it a try.

At that time, I didn't know anyone in San Diego so I thought I'd try to see if I could stay in a place where the other person was actually there and rent a private room, not an entire apartment. I started to research a few spots. My requirements were pretty basic: maybe watch some football at a bar, possibly catch a Padres game. I was basically trying to use Airbnb to find a friend, since I did not know one person in all of California.

I saw this guy's picture and he was wearing an Indians jersey at a baseball game; he was a guy from Cleveland, Cameron Eckstein. He seemed "normal," which could not be further from the truth (love you, Cam). So I booked a room at his home. Now he's my best friend in San Diego *and* we're partners in our Airbnb ventures.

My first Airbnb experience turned out all right.

I stayed in San Diego about a year-and-a-half before I prepared to move to Austin, Texas, where I lived for nine months. The thing was, I still needed to go back to San Diego once a month, for a week or so. I was part of a group called Entrepreneurs' Organization (formerly Young Entrepreneurs) and this group meant (and means) a lot to me. My EO forum consists of me and seven married guys with kids, but I would not trade them for anyone in the world. The criteria to get in required showing a proven level of success with a million-dollar minimum in revenue, and you must be the CEO or founder of your company. These forums rock. You learn so much from them every month when they take place. I now consider it a fundamental part of my continued growth in business, family, and personal life.

Cameron and I saw an opportunity that presented an idea to partner up and buy a property in San Diego—one that I could Airbnb out when I wasn't there. It made sense. He'd manage the property for the standard 20 percent management fee (this is the universal fee as of the writing of this book), so he'd make some money, and I could make some money and have a place to stay for free when I was in town.

This seemed too good to be true. As we all know, you can write off depreciation, taxes, and interest. Plus, real estate, just like the stock market, always goes up over time.

So we went for it and it has worked out well. Now I am at Superhost status and I have an occupancy rate of over 85 percent.

From what we've seen and the research I've conducted, there is a massive opportunity for growth with Airbnb that exists today. Maybe not in twenty years, but today it is single-handedly the best low-risk investment out there. We've begun seeking other properties using some of the software companies that have sprung up that are specific to Airbnb (Mashvisor and AirDNA, for example). You pay money for a zip code and access a plethora of data that they've already scrubbed out pertaining to Airbnb specifically. It's a time-saver and a decision-maker. Airbnb makes sense for me because just like trading it is a mathematical equation. We will go to these details in a later chapter, but it is all about the occupancy rate, average room rate, and cash-on-cash return, *baby*.

Our next destination is a property in Arizona, in Old Town Scottsdale. It's turnkey, and the data for profitability in that area is spot-on with the goals for growth that we have. We look at 12 percent-18 percent cash-on-cash return, not including the tax write-offs we have talked about, money that goes toward principal, and the hidden gem: leverage and appreciation.

How did we do it? I'll break it down for you later, but the formula isn't rocket science in this case. There are specific variables you take into consideration and from there, you act or take a pass.

Today, I have a large presence for the Airbnb model and continue to teach others just like I taught them on trading about the Airbnb business models. I can be seen or heard on:

- ▶ Social media
- ▶ Podcasts
- ▶ Interviews
- ▶ Television
- ▶ Anyone at Starbucks or even the bar who wants to learn about it

What I've shared has been noticed. I've always gotten random calls from my public presence about various reality shows. Some crazier than you would ever get me to say yes to. Things like *Married by Mom and Dad* on TLC or *Dating Naked* on VH1. I helped write a book with a good friend, Justin Robinson, called *Look Amazing Naked*, but no, not for TV, thanks.

One day I received a call about another reality show. Skepticism entered my mind, but I always give people a chance, so I listened. Would it be crazy shit like it was most often...yet to be determined?

I scheduled a time to talk with this woman for thirty minutes and an hour plus later, we're still on the phone. As my brother says, I love talking to myself. It's a reality show, but it's one that I definitely am interested in. It's for an Airbnb show for CNBC (an unreal opportunity and I would drop almost anything to work with CNBC) and the concept is to work with an interior designer and go through the process and numbers of purchasing a property for Airbnb rental from beginning to end. I'm one of about twenty they are considering. They'd seen some TV appearance I'd made on Airbnb and, for lack of a better term, I passed their initial "stink test."

This woman's talking about all these things and I am just trying to be myself, which is I'm quite the character. I'm talking and saying, "Put twelve drinks in me and you will have no idea what I am going to say next."

Then she asked if she could set me up with her best friend in Los Angeles for a date. I Googled the friend, and I passed, but I appreciated the thought. I did not think much of the interview so I forgot to follow up until about a month passed by, I think. Then I got a call and she told me that they had loved the interview. I was still in contention.

Now things were feeling very real.

Next was another interview, this time with her producer.

My assistant and I began a research blitz and pulled up every stat and bit of information about Airbnb we could find. If searching the internet were a game, I think I would win at it. Who needs Watson when I have me? I memorized it and took it in. Having these bits of information and lots of one-liners on hand to share is an important part of television appearances. I have done so many TV hits that this is easy for me. I feel very comfortable about any question anyone would ever ask me. For example, "Airbnb's most profitable cities for properties are in Miami and San Diego." Or, "The city of Paris has the most Airbnb listings." I was now the established expert and I had to be prepared to share some great details and answer any pop questions. I'm confident when faced by a good challenge, so bring it on.

During this time, I learned about the way TV shows work. Some producers come up with a concept and pitch it to a network and then they come up with a supporting cast. They say "yes" or "no" and then a mock trailer is created for the buyer. If the trailer gets picked up, you're in. If only it were as easy as it sounded.

The time for the interview came and the casting agency producer who I'm to talk with wants it as much as me, I think. He's prepping me and telling me the guy I'm speaking with will not show a lot of emotion, but I should just go for it. I'll be fine. I was ready, down to knowing where the CNBC producer lived and various details that would interest him, and I threw it all out there, throwing stats specific to his area and drawing him in.

As the interview ended, I began to talk about other things that were important to me, such as socially responsible companies. Giving back is a part of the legacy I'm building, because I've had a really blessed life and I get that. I say, "It would be cool to do a concept with Airbnb where we give some of the profits of the show back to charity, maybe building houses in Africa or something."

I wait.

He responds. "Yeah, we wouldn't do that."

Well, okay then.

I am so excited and pumped that I did something crazy that I am not sure has worked out yet. I handwrote two letters to both CNBC producers, had them overnighted to Englewood, New Jersey, and discussed how I will work twenty hours a day, sleep under a desk, and do *anything* in my power to make this show a crazy success.

After the interview, I'm talking to the guy in Cali and he asks how it went. "About a B-," I said. The same grade I got in Astronomy 100. Then I explained the social awareness and he responded by saying, "Gee, that's just called being a good person." Moral of the story: when talking to people in California, do as the Californians do and when you are talking to people from the East Coast, I need to bring out my crazy aggressive side.

Thankfully, there was good news. He added that if they picked it up they wanted me to be the investor. It went from twenty people to me and only me, which is crazy to think. I mean, I have written now five books and eight e-books, and I think I would kill it on TV because I am raw and unfiltered, but actually speak very well and properly.

Now I was officially in the "my-hopes-are-up" stage. I wanted this show—bad.

A few days later he tells me that they @#$% love me. They've seen all my work and they're sold.

A week later I get the word that it's happening. I'm getting the trailer.

"How does this work?" I ask.

I get word that I'll shoot a trailer in July 2017. It'll take about a week, and if they pick it up, we'll have an eight-episode season, one in prime time. If the show does well, it's renewed.

All this is going on and the book you're reading now was one that I'd been talking about more than taking action to write. But the time for action has come, my friend. Airbnb is big enough that they want a TV show featuring how it works on a financial network. That's a big deal. I am still waiting and waiting on the contract and I think that it will come. However, I am a big believer that if it is meant to be, then it will happen and if it is not meant to be, then it won't. This is about fate, destiny, and believing that everything happens for a reason. Heck, I'm almost thirty-eight and single; I have to believe in this.

Now I'm committed to this, vested emotionally, and I can just see it playing out. I'm excited.

Another week goes by and I hear word that there is a contract for me, my "name already on it" type of contract. I want to see it, of course, and then my next big lesson in TV deals unfolds.

He can't show me. That's policy. It goes back and forth between lawyers. But don't worry...the show won't happen without me. I'm the "chosen one" for it.

Okay, so send it to me, I say.

I'm still waiting.

Maybe this is how TV works, but it's not how Airbnb works. Throughout this book I am going to teach you everything I have learned about Airbnb from various courses I've taken, from every book on the subject that I've read, and from personal experience. Please enjoy reading this book as much as I like talking.

Are you ready to dive into what it takes to be a forty-niner in the 21st-century goldmine?

What the California Gold Rush Taught Us

"During the Gold Rush, most would-be miners lost money,
but those who sold them picks, shovels, tents and blue-jeans
(Levi Strauss) made a nice profit."

— PETER LYNCH —

Without the California Gold Rush there wouldn't have been a California, at least not as quickly. Imagine the year 1848, and the territory of California is there. Adventurers and explorers are pioneering new trails and looking for new opportunities.

During any time frame, a smart investor has to figure out *a)* what the new and great opportunity is, and *b)* how you can use arbitrage and make money from the opportunity. This is why I call Airbnb a modern-day goldmine.

Imagine what it was like...prospectors coming across something big...*gold*. They're excited and get to work becoming miners and prospectors. The word gets out and quickly catches on. We are not at that point yet. People still don't realize the opportunity that Airbnb represents.

Eventually for the Gold Rush crowd it is 1849 and a mad rush to the California territory ensues. Everyone is interested in getting their piece of that golden opportunity. It's not even a state yet; that didn't happen until 1850.

**Depending on your vision, you looked at California
at that time and either saw it for its gold,
or as a goldmine to supply the prospectors
with what they needed to make it a success.**

Now there's a frenzy going on and people from all over the United States, nearby territories, and even other countries are paying attention. This is what you *must realize* when you think of possible alternative investments such as Airbnb. I think of it as an investor, first and foremost. There are basically four decisions that they can make.

- ▶ Take advantage of the opportunity while it's still a hot iron.
- ▶ Say no to the risk because it isn't appealing.
- ▶ Wait a bit and see if it keeps going strong, and then make your move.
- ▶ Say, "Heck, I have nothing to lose so I should jump on the opportunity quickly and fast, before other people realize how great this prospect could be."

Regardless of what you decide, what is happening in California won't be stopped. It's a new world. Towns, outposts, and mines need to be built. Commerce has to be established and services provided to this crazy influx of new people into the territory. With all these things comes what people really want—money. People want to make money.

There are two great quotes I love when people talk about money. The first is, "Money doesn't make you happy." While I totally believe this is true, it really implies that just because someone has money does not mean they are happy. The other quote is, "People who say money doesn't buy happiness has never lived my life." This is a favorite because while money does not buy happiness, it does make everything in life better.

Life is easier with money and this is why people continue to do anything in their power to achieve it: kill, murder, and steal.

The people who made the most money during the Gold Rush were those who either took:

- ▶ **Option One**—taking advantage of the opportunity while it was hot.
- ▶ **Option Two**—looking beyond the prospectors and miners, and into what they would need to achieve their ambitions.

In a speculative phase of a hot industry, whether it be a goldmine of the 1850s or the current Airbnb goldmine of 2010s, an investor must find the best way to make money, and investing the way I will teach you in this book will help you navigate through this.

Looking beyond the draw of the gold and into what it took to build the towns, housing, stores, outposts, saloons, and schools was opportunity. Finding ways to make and offer the clothing, tools, supplies, and other staples was opportunity. This is the key you must remember and repeat to yourself daily if you are looking for any alternative investments—where are my opportunities to make money? Basically, if you had the foresight, will, and desire, you had a chance for success.

To put it into perspective, it's estimated that miners earned about twenty dollars a day, but those who provided the supplies and services those miners needed were looking at about five thousand dollars a day (today, this equates to approximately 125,000 dollars a day).

The way people responded emotionally to the California Gold Rush is something that still exists today, all over the world. You just have to find it.

We are always going to have trailblazers, people willing to commit right away, those who will always pass, and those who can see beyond the initial draw of any opportunity. That's the name of the game.

I always say that there are two types of people in this world: people who get it and people who don't. This is also true of business. Some people will talk about their dreams, and others will follow theirs. I am one of those people who will drop everything to follow my dreams, passions, and goals even if they are not that profitable and hard to find at first.

I want you to do something that is different than what you normally do. Try a new hobby or adventure, or start that business that you always wanted to, even if it costs money, time, energy, effort, and stress. Ideas are endless, and everywhere.

Levi Strauss created denim so he could make durable jeans with riveted pockets that would not tear for miners. Today, jeans are one of the most popular types of clothing someone can purchase—including Levis!

In California, four Sacramento merchants known as "The Big Four" tapped into the market for hardware stores and grocery stores. These names were Charles Crocker, Mark Hopkins, Collis P. Huntington, and Leland Stanford. With the money they earned they changed the face of transportation in a significant way by creating a transcontinental railroad dynasty. This took place during the beginning of the Gold Rush and it shows an important lesson—every couple of decades a big opportunity likely arrives and you alone must realize what it is or be left in the dust.

An impressive 465 million dollars was infused into the national economy due to the California Gold Rush.

The Gold Rush was a big boom that changed the landscape of opportunity in America. Consider these numbers:

- ▶ In 1849, ten million dollars' worth of gold was extracted.
- ▶ Just two years later, in 1851, that number increased to seventy-five million dollars.
- ▶ And in 1852, it was eighty-one million dollars.

In addition to economic success, there was also an infusion of different cultures from across the world that changed the social landscape of California. Initially, Sam Brannan had moved to the territory in hopes of establishing a Mormon community. Then he saw gold, and a diverse group of people arrived, all interested in the same thing—earning money and having an opportunity. A new start, for many more people.

Then it eventually began to die down. The mining industry was oversaturated and the supply and demand dwindled. We are not at this point of the Airbnb business model for an investor, and this is a much greater opportunity than the Gold Rush was. There is great potential for Airbnb worldwide, not just in California. Every single person in the world can make money on Airbnb, either from renting their entire house, every room, or even a shared room. Airbnb founders Joe Gebbia and Brian Chesky have stated multiple times that the demand from customers is greater than the demand from suppliers with properties.

Are you wondering what happens and who suffers during a downturn? In California, the first to suffer from the economic downturn were the miners. Their daily earnings fell to less than six dollars a day, which equated to more than a two-thirds drop from what they'd earned in 1848 when the Gold Rush began.

This entire story of the California Gold Rush is wrought with parallels to what Airbnb is today. The people who got onboard first with this innovative way to book homes from local hosts when you travel are seeing exceptional returns on their investments. Those who cater to the needs that Airbnb hosts have now have a niche that has gained them access to selling their services that make the job of hosting easier.

What we know for sure is all this will come to an end some day. *When* is yet to be determined, but these opportunities are cyclical. They don't last forever. As stated, the iron is hot, so you must hit *now*.

Many times, there is no rhyme or reason why something is such a hot commodity one day and not the next. It just happens as interests shift and innovations come forward. As I speak, Bitcoin and crypto currencies are another hot way where money could be made.

As a trader, I love delving into the analytics of why certain things perform the way they do, and it is often evident that part of it rides on emotion; as the years pass by, peoples' desires shift. Today, people want experiences, and there's no better way to have an experience than to travel. I have been to forty-nine of the 196 countries in the world and I am planning trips to Columbia, Fiji, and China as we speak. Even if your travel is for business only, you likely want a better travel experience.

The value of experiences is hard to fully appreciate. There has been evidence of certain things being perceived as valuable around for all of time.

Tulipmania was one of the first rushes. In the Netherlands in the 1640s, tulips were used as currency. You could even purchase a house with them. It now seems crazy that you could buy a house with tulips, but think about it, this is exactly what gold represents.

Consider why gold became so valuable. It has zero industrial use, and the United States has been off the gold standard since President Nixon was president. Its first appeal was in using it instead of cash when traveling. It made sense to carry a single coin versus a bunch of currency.

How about diamonds? Why are they worth so much? They are not a rare gem. A ruby is a rare gem, yet DeBeers created a diamond market that makes them valuable. It could crash if diamonds weren't so linked to wedding and engagement rings.

I used to visit comic book and baseball shows with my father when I was a younger teenager. Why was it that a Michael Jordan rookie card was worth a thousand bucks? This was once again a simple supply and demand curve for a product—more aggressive a buyer's price goes higher; more aggressive a seller's price goes lower. Think about it, the card had Jordon's picture and some information printed on cardboard, but it was in high demand. Eventually this market did crash.

Think about water. It's finite, not infinite, yet it sells for 50 cents at the store for a bottled water. Why is that? That same bottle of water is worth 50 cents, one dollar for one bottle from a street vendor, but seven dollars at the Cubs game. It's the same bottle of water; nothing has changed except the location of where you purchase that bottle of water.

If you're uncertain about the opportunities of Airbnb because you're feeling uncertain of its long-term potential, understand that nothing lasts forever. The best investments don't take place at the end of the trend, but the beginning. You have to make a decision: you're either in or you're not. If you wait too long, time has proven that you're likely to get disappointing results.

To master Airbnb, you need to understand the trend, the emotions, real estate, and what is required to master hosting. All this information is covered in what you're reading right now and this book will teach you everything you need to master Airbnb.

Are you going to take action today and make money and become an Airbnb host?

Are you going to think of all the services that can help those who are hosts make their investments more valuable to their clients?

Are you going to take a pass and hope to catch the next trend immediately, whenever that may happen?

Imagine what you could do in your life if you never worried about fear, failing, and what other people would think of you. So many people in this world are scared of failure when they shouldn't be.

What you do is not necessarily going to be a bad choice, but it does come with a consequence. For you it may mean that you won't be able to profit from this 21st century gold mine.

2

The Changing
Real Estate Horizon

"In the middle of every difficulty lies opportunity."

— ALBERT EINSTEIN —

Airbnb is so unique because it has tapped into the real estate industry in a manner that has not been previously explored. Airbnb is not the first company in this field, but through its platform, word of mouth, and hard work it has become the industry leader. It has created an emotional experience for consumers with a profitability model for those who own real estate.

Understanding the history of real estate helps you to better understand the foundation of real estate investing, along with the significant events over time that are a big part of the history of how it has changed over the years.

One thing you can be assured of with real estate is that it will always be necessary. Unlike gold, diamonds, or even tulips, people must live with a roof over their heads. The markets may fluctuate due to supply and demand issues, but people need places to live, and owning property is still one of the most profitable endeavors you can invest in—if you do it right.

The real estate market is very similar to the U.S. stock market, where prices will always go up over time. Also, there are major advantages to real estate that include interest, taxes, and depreciation. To take advantage of this fully, you should talk to a real estate tax expert, which I am not.

The Great Depression of 1929

From the beginning of September 1929 through the end of October that year the U.S. real estate market took a significant downturn, losing 40 percent of its value. Imagine having one hundred thousand dollars in the bank and then in two months forty thousand dollars of that is gone. Crazy to think, but market corrections do happen about every year at about a rate of a 10 percent correction every five years. But it is crazy to think about a 40 percent correction.

The people who are alive today who lived through the Depression can attest to how bad they thought that moment in time was. Then they learned that wasn't even the bottoming-out point. This didn't happen until July 1932 and that 40 percent had reached a staggering 90 percent.

I always say when I am trading that volatility creates opportunity as a trader.

To put this into perspective, according to the S&P Corelogic Case-Shiller U.S. National Home Price Index, which Robert Shiller helped to create, the average cost of a home then was six thousand dollars. By 1932, that had dropped to one thousand dollars. Because of this, just like stocks became a part of the plights of the Great Depression, so did housing. So they may have referred to "depression" as an economic turn, but you can imagine the amount of real depression that people experienced. Most weren't in the stock market so that crash didn't impact them. The number of people who invested in the stock market during that time was way different than the numbers of people who currently invest in it.

However, this was a time when many people were still farmers and they were already facing struggles due to decreased prices for their goods. When a market crashes, either stocks or real estate, it affects more than just the people in those markets. It affects pricing of goods, unemployment, and the whole economy.

Four thousand-plus banks closed during the Great Depression and there were two million homeless people living in the United States. At that time, there were approximately 123 million people in the U.S.

With this significant drop in real estate, those who were able to look into the future and realize that the market would take an upturn again began to strategize. This is how you should be looking at the Airbnb potential right now. Twelve years ago, any idiot and their mother could flip a house. Buy it for seventy thousand dollars, put thirty thousand dollars into it, and six months later sell it for 130,000 dollars. This is much harder right now and one of the reasons why is that as times change, investors must change their investment strategies. Despite what it may feel like through the retelling of history, not everyone is negatively impacted in even the most tumultuous economic times. Some people see the opportunity that is present even in tough times, as well as in preparing for when things begin to rebound. As we have studied, we are the dominate country of the world and corrections set up for bounces, and over time the bounces are much stronger than the initial sell-off.

Despite a lack of money, areas that offered an emotional reprieve, such as movies, music, and baseball, didn't see the same financial woes as the rest of the economy. Babe Ruth made eighty thousand dollars a year (which equates to one million dollars a year today). Movie theaters did suffer significant dips in revenues, down to a net of 480 million dollars in 1933. Many theaters did close their doors; however, many also became resourceful to keep their seats filled. They'd have promotions to fill those seats and it worked. By 1941 movie ticket revenues had climbed back up to 810 million dollars. There are stocks that are known as addiction stocks or recessionary stocks. No matter how bad the economy may be, people will always smoke, drink alcohol, and gamble. Addiction stock... it makes sense, doesn't it? You have to release stress somewhere, even if it isn't the healthiest.

Astute businesspeople also realize that even in the toughest of times there are basic needs that people have which cannot be eliminated. Procter & Gamble took advantage of this by committing to unique marketing that made them the ideal choice when buying soap. Through their unique marketing efforts, they created serial shows on the radio to draw in housewives. It offered entertainment and pushed their product. Today, these serials are known as soap operas. Never underestimate how a bit of ingenuity and creative marketing can go a long way. This is the ways of thinking in the life of an entrepreneur. Airbnb has participated in this, connecting people emotionally to real estate and experiences.

Utilities were another area still necessary despite the Great Depression. Floyd Bostwick Odlum was a corporate attorney who didn't assume the stock market would last forever, unlike many who had the luxury of being able to invest in it. He took his money out of the market and had the valuable commodity of cold hard cash before the Depression hit. This reminds me of another quote I love: "Cash is king."

Yes, the type of investing you do with the Airbnb business model could yield up to 30 percent a year, but with higher reward there is always higher risk. Real estate could take a major dip again at any time and those who have cash to allocate can always take advantage of this dip. When the dip happened, it was not a surprise for which Odlum was unprepared. He was prepared to stand in when others couldn't. He began to buy utility companies, turning thirty-seven thousand dollars into a fortune that made him the richest man in America for a period of time.

The last people to really thrive during the Great Depression were the ones who catered to the needs of the people who did not like to be told what to do by others. Specifically, Prohibition. Brewing beer for people during this time made brewers some of the richest people in the country. Life is stressful. People have and will always have to take the edge off and they do this through drugs and alcohol. I like to indulge in a beer or twelve every couple of nights as well.

These lessons and insights show us another example of how there is always an opportunity in even the craziest-looking scenario. Positioning yourself to get in during ideal times is how you can make a lot of money. And with that money you have the potential to do a lot of good for people and offer people what they need, not just what they want. This is the main reason that I am writing this book—to let you know that Airbnb is this type of opportunity and I can teach you all about hosting, using it as a customer, and investing in it.

1940s: A Suburban Boom

With the improved methods of available transportation, creation of more roadways, and the post-war boom, there was an adjustment into the areas where people chose to live. Not staying right in the cities or towns became an option, and there were many eager takers for suburbia. Why? Land was a lot more affordable.

My grandfather was one of these men. He'd had a lot of businesses in his life and most of them had failed. But he still managed to have money, perhaps the result of being a guy who went through the Great Depression. It taught the value of saving and living within your means during that era to a great many people. He lived in Wisconsin, near Milwaukee, and he took note of people heading toward the suburbs in droves.

He did some research and chose to purchase some land near Milwaukee in a place that is now known as Mequon, with an average home value of 371,400 dollars as of this date and a population of over 23,000. At the time of Grandpa's purchase, it was farmland that at 20 miles seemed obscenely far away from Milwaukee. It was isolated as hell, and a great many people thought he was crazy, but his hunch and understanding of the trend proved to be quite different. Grandpa was smart and intuitive about the world and it paid off.

Recognizing patterns and trends is a part of the reason I have been so successful in my trading career. This can be true of anyone in any industry. Chris Sacca is a guy worth over one billion dollars and an example of this. His firm made early investments in Twilio, Twitter, Instagram, and Uber. Is he just lucky? Hell no; he has an eye for great start-ups.

Through my brief time in real estate and through learning from some of the best real estate investors in the world I have learned enough to write an encyclopedia. I've extracted the "must know points" for you to get your act together and bring out your innovator and financial creator through the Airbnb model.

As the Big Boom to the suburbs began people all over the United States saw opportunities to purchase a larger home for a fraction of the price in the suburbs compared to purchasing a home for triple the price and a third of the size in the city. It was an easy choice for many to make.

Buying the land to help people recognize this opportunity was where the business-minded visionaries stood apart. While some investors still did very well with investing in properties in the city, the ones with this great eye for future trends received much larger rates of return by investing in suburbs as opposed to the city. They were meeting a need and offering something appealing to a large portion of the population. Life was just getting easier and the economy was booming again. It was a great period of growth, as post-war times most always are. Purchasing land made sense. It gained value and offered a great rate of return for the people who got there first.

As a successful trader, I have made millions of dollars trading. As Kevin O'Leary from CNBC's *Shark Tank* has put it: *"I look at this money as soldiers and their goal is to bring back more soldiers."* I want to put my money through work, but I also do not want to lose money. So, my goal is to put the money to work. With the ten-year bond through the government, my goal is to put my money in places where I can make more money. However, it is a numbers game and this is where I excel. Would I rather get 2 percent returns and have a 100 percent guarantee of my money or a 20 percent return with an 80 percent guarantee of my money? This is so obvious to me that every single investment I make involves weighing the risk versus return factor. The Airbnb business model right now is the best reward to risk setup I have *ever* seen. This is why I am taking so much time, energy, and effort to teach the concepts to you.

Getting there first is directly aligned with the profit margin you can get in any hot commodity.

Think of modern-day San Diego. Aside from growing upward, there is only one other direction it can grow if it wishes to expand, and that is to the east. If you go west you'll encounter an obstacle called the ocean. If you go north, you're looking at the highway. Going south doesn't really work because of a little issue called the border. So east it is. In San Diego, 10th Avenue and Park used to be undesirable, but right now it is hot. Developers are using this to expand east and quickly.

Because of its eastward growth, sections of San Diego that were once considered the ghettos are now becoming revitalized areas. Housing values are going up and everything is shifting. Real estate in the past three years has appreciated 8 percent, 11 percent, and 13 percent. By the power of leverage anyone can take advantage of this. Let's say that you buy a place for five hundred thousand dollars and you put down 20 percent or one hundred thousand dollars; then, if the real estate value appreciated 10 percent you would be making fifty thousand dollars a year on that one hundred thousand dollars or 50 percent not including the potential 20 percent cash-on-cash return (which you'll learn later). *This is a 70 percent return.* Where else in the world can anyone get this type of return without it being illegal or risky? It demonstrates another opportunity for foresight into future trends. Even purchasing in the depressed areas of a city a few years ago can lead to revitalizing properties that are ideal for Airbnb hosting, as well as holding other investment purposes.

The key is to do what it takes to be on the cutting edge. Research and know what's going on in any place you want to invest in.

When I learned about this through Airbnb I did the first thing possible to understand it better and that was to read every single Airbnb book on the market. From my point of view, which is always skewed a little bit, this book you're reading right now is the *only book* that teaches you the history of real estate, the reasons why to invest in real estate, and then dives into secrets and details of being a host. If you want to master anything, it is not that hard; pick up a book and read.

Busted: The 2007–2008 Real Estate Market

Let's start with a story that happened from the famous movie and book by Michael Lewis, *The Big Short*. A group of guys in the movie were visiting Florida for some business and went to a strip club. Being a housing guy, one asked one of the ladies how many houses she owned. She replied, "Five houses and a condo." He had to ask why. Her response was "because she could." That's when they knew that when this housing bubble burst, it was going to burst hard.

Not everyone gets their realization from colorful ladies dancing the catwalk, but it demonstrates the fact that people want to jump in on a good thing to make money, and if it's easy to do, why not do it.

For the most part, the mentality about real estate was that even with up and down markets, real estate was a fairly safe investment. This is the exact same way the stock market works. Throughout history the stock market has always gone up over time, but that does not mean that there aren't periods where corrections will happen. During this time, those people who are not well educated will lose money.

Before the "bust" people were encouraged to buy a home and as they paid down on it they were building up a valuable, resalable asset. This was true. However, the big bust of the real estate bubble from 2007–2008 shattered this belief for many people. It was startling, if not unexpected, by a majority of people that it impacted. Everything had been looking good for so long that it seemed like real estate was some type of god—invincible. Welcome, the Achilles heel.

This entire debacle, which was devastating to so many people, was a slow buildup that was a result of policies and regulations over a period of maybe twenty years. They made it so easy for people to buy houses on credit because "homes" always go up. This would be very similar to being able to buy one million dollars' worth of AAPL stock for one hundred thousand dollars. Well, look at a stock chart of AAPL; the stock always goes higher. I think most people would do that thinking that if the stock goes higher they could pay that money back. Well, what if AAPL stock plummeted and went down and you still owed money on the one million dollars' worth of stock you bought? You would be in a world of hurt.

At first, just like with most regulations, it seemed good. In the end, it proved disastrous.

A few key points include:

▸ **Ben Bernanke** (former Chairman of the Federal Reserve) said a factor for the burst was the inflow of foreign savings into the U.S. economy.

▸ **Yuliya Demyanyk** (head of macro research at Man Ahl in London) and Otto Van Hemert (former assistant professor, NYU) determined that there had been deterioration in the quality of subprime loans for six-plus years. Subprime loans are loans offered to individuals who don't meet standard requirements for traditional loans. The reason that these loans were given is because mortgage lenders make money off commissions. So they were giving out huge numbers of loans to get a huge commission check. They got the reward and tens of thousands of Americans lost their life savings and went bankrupt. A lot of people got shafted from not understanding.

▶ **Jon Leibowitz** (former Chairman of the Federal Trade Commission) mentioned how government had played a role in the weakening mortgage underwriting standards so that when real estate growth stopped defaults increased.

One of the few major downfalls of the Airbnb system that I am going to teach you is the fact that it is so hard to get a loan nowadays. It's crazy hard, more than you could ever imagine until you try. Or maybe you don't try because of the crappy stories you hear from guys like me.

Let me tell you what you have to go through when your finances are in pretty good shape. Every single deposit and withdrawal has to be accounted for. I even had to have my CPA sign a letter that stated if I took one hundred thousand dollars out of my business to buy a unit that it wouldn't affect my business from going out of business. Insane, and if you have even a slightly weak constitution, stressful. And you have to do what they request. Your investment kind of depends on it.

With policies and regulations that set people up for a potential disaster everything was bound to come to a boiling point. Many investors purchased properties with hopes of getting great returns on them, both as their primary residences, and as investment properties. Rates were low and ARM products (adjustable rate mortgages) became popular.

As an example:

> If you borrowed two hundred thousand dollars on a 3/1 ARM at a rate of 3 percent, you'd be looking at a starting payment of 843.21 dollars of Principle & Interest (P&I). This would last for three years and then the rate fluctuates depending on the market. A typical cap would be 2 percent up or down of that starting rate of 3 percent per year.
>
> Assume that the rate goes up the full 2 percent on the fourth year. This creates a P&I payment of 1,053.38 dollars. This is almost a 25 percent increase in the price of your mortgage. This is a big difference, especially if taxes and insurance go up too. Can you see why this would create so many problems for a great many consumers? Rent demand rates don't necessarily go up just because interest rates do. And for primary residences, the difference in payment can be a significant added expense to some families. Most people in the United States live paycheck to paycheck so this increase is huge for them. Imagine the impact if they had more than one property.

Now consider this example with a fixed rate loan:

> You borrow two hundred thousand dollars on a thirty-year fixed rate of 7 percent. You're looking at a starting P&I payment of 1,331.00 dollars, knowing that rate will never adjust. Taxes and insurance might, but not your P&I.

In summary, all these factors ultimately made it so that it was a tough time for most people to own real estate for the long haul, especially if they took advantage of subprime lending services, which may use higher qualifying ratios, undocumented loans (no evidence of assets or income), and less money down on property prices that were teetering on their highest point.

But again, people who understood the trends and went about investing in a more conservative manner were able to survive this burst bubble, which is still in recovery to this day. I tell my traders many times that the only thing better than making money in a trade is not losing money in a bad trade. I call it sitting on my hands during the day. This means that I am only looking for the best possible trades, not trading just to make trades. As the prices plummeted, their ability to buy low went up. This is one of the reasons that people refer to this time period as the Great Recession. We weren't as bad off as people were during the Great Depression, but we were impacted.

> **Today, no matter how stellar your credit is or what type of income you can prove you make, banks ask for explanations on just about everything.**

New regulations such as Dodd-Frank have created many changes to bank lending practices. Even my friends who were killing it as mortgage lenders have been affected because they are not making nearly as much money as they were. The number of qualified loans has reduced significantly. It was necessary because of the big bailouts all those banks had to take because of all the subprime lending disasters. To keep it simple, banks were forced by government to do these types of loans and then had to be bailed out by the government for doing them. Yeah, it's as crazy as it seems.

Today, those who began investing in the properties that were in distress or that consumers had to return to lenders are seeing another upswing of real estate values starting. Once again—another movie reference—but in *Wall Street: Money Never Sleeps* this is what the famous Gordon Gecko did. I know it is fiction and a movie, but he loaded up on cash on the side and then when it was time to buy he did and made millions in the process.

Lending is now more controlled and regulated, but still filled with opportunity. This rebound rides perfectly on the wave of a rising, in-demand service known as Airbnb. Some of the best businesses and opportunities are a result of timing Let's be honest, everything in life is about timing, not just business but relationships as well.

The Death of Flipping

The people who flip houses are like those who provided services to the miners and prospectors during the California Gold Rush. They were able to go in and swoop up distressed properties cheap, make some improvements, and sell them for a great return. Even though I personally did not do this, I have talked to many friends who did. This was easy to do, but unless you have pocket listings or deals that you can pay in all cash, this is a dead business model. It did fit two needs:

1. Revitalization in distressed areas
2. Making a lot of money with quick turnover properties

Then it became overly saturated with speculators who were not really interested in repairing the properties, but buying them and selling them right away for a bit more money. When this happened, everyone was able to do this. It became a full-time job for some people and before you knew it, too many people were doing the same thing. Any time that an industry gets too crowded and there is not much of a barrier of entry the market will become saturated and it makes it too hard to make money.

Suddenly properties weren't selling as fast—goodbye days of multiple offers lined up within twenty-four hours—and shit hit the ceiling. Payments began coming due that couldn't be made. Renters were going into these properties, but the going rental rates were lower than the payments. Hell, rental payments were not even made to the lender, but simply pocketed by the now distressed landlord. Goes to show, simple isn't always sensational. This easy spiral affected everything.

So, nothing more needs to be said about this than, "Goodbye to the days of flipping. They are long gone."

Airbnb: An Exciting New Option

Today is the hottest day for Airbnb. Not tomorrow or the next day—today! Not being dramatic, just being practical. Airbnb is the largest privately held company in the world that is profitable and I believe that it will have an IPO in the fall of 2018.

The evidence of how these trends move has been laid out for you. Because of the demand that Airbnb has met to date, it is a serious contender for everyone who is serious about earning money and leveraging their real estate investments. Airbnb has stated multiple times that the demand is much larger than the supply and we will teach you the reasons why this is in the next couple of chapters.

Airbnb is a disrupter that can be an investment saver. Even if you can't rent an investment property any longer, if you do things right, you can sell it and make a bit of money. Or you can consider the Airbnb model and either cut your losses, break even, or even build equity and cover your payment.

Why It's Smart
to Consider Airbnb

*"Certainly the advent of technology and electronic
commerce has had an immense impact
on the real estate industry."*

— MICHAEL OXLEY —

You're considering being an Airbnb host, and it is a big decision. A lot depends on it, including:

▶ If you currently own a property in a marketable area. I will teach you that even if you live in Deerfield, Illinois—where my parents live—every single city is a marketable city.

▶ The city and area you live in, specifically its rules and ordinances regarding short-term rentals (which Airbnb rentals often are). Some cities such as New York have banned short-term rentals.

▶ A thorough assessment of the risks involved in opening your property to people you do not know. There is a one million dollar-guarantee insurance policy through Airbnb, but you must understand what is covered and not covered in this policy.

It all seems complicated, but it does not have to be. The decision-making process relies upon sound information, and understanding what the experience may be. This leads me to my first tip for you:

> **Tip #1: Try staying at an Airbnb property from a Superhost to see what it's like, and how the experience feels as a consumer.**

In 2007 two roommates living in San Francisco were having a few financial struggles and they needed to figure a way to make their rent. What if they threw a few air mattresses down in their living room and just charged people to sleep there? This is what they thought. At the time it seemed like a crazy idea; I mean, who the @#$% would want to sleep on an air mattress in a living room? For them, the need was simple. Doing this would give them some cash to pay their rent and that would help. Throw in breakfast and it might be even better. After all, creative people know that often enough it's the craziest seeming ideas that actually work.

In this thought, Airbnb was born: Air-bed-n-breakfast.

These two guys trying to make ends meet were Brian Chesky and Joe Gebbia. What began as a discussion on how to pay the bills caught fire and began growing rapidly. As with most businesses, it wasn't an overnight success and there were many struggles, such as funding, but these two were hard workers willing to do anything to make their idea and business work.

Today, Airbnb is a decade old, and is found in 191 countries out of 196. And paying the rent has converted itself into a privately owned business that nets one billion dollars-plus per year. According to Reuters, the revenue for Airbnb increased by 80 percent in 2016. You don't have to be a financial guru to know that 80 percent growth is more than average, it's practically unheard of. This shows why this is one of the hottest industries. Airbnb wasn't the first to do it, but can you easily name a competitor? There are various reasons Airbnb is the best and they will be highlighted in this book.

> **Tip #2:** When paying rent for one apartment turns into three million housing listings in 65,000 cities, you should probably pay attention. The bonus: these numbers increase every day.

Are you thinking, this isn't for me? Maybe it's not, but make sure you do your due diligence before you jump to that conclusion, especially if you're someone who talks about taking strategic chances to accumulate wealth.

Here are a few thoughts to guide you in having a thoughtful evaluation of Airbnb, as a whole:

▶ Renting out an extra room to help pay your mortgage
▶ Paying for your European vacation by renting out your whole house
▶ The arbitrage situation on renting out long term rentals and moving them to short term rentals
▶ Buying units for the 20% cash on cash return plus appreciation and tax write-offs.

If any of these thoughts sound in line with goals and desires you have, Airbnb can provide—if you learn how to host effectively.

Big Questions, Insightful Answers

Here are some of the most popular questions that people ask when they begin the process.

Who Is Likely to Rent My Place?

Some hosts rent to anyone who can afford the price. It's an individual decision based on their goals. The most common people to whom hosts cater include:

- ▶ Party people: group of good friends
- ▶ Families taking vacations
- ▶ Business travelers

And now, Airbnb has other options that interest people. They are constantly thinking and innovating ways to introduce your property to the world. These include:

- ▶ Experiences, which are opportunities to rent your place out and offer a fun or unique experience to the renters (more in the hosting chapter). This is currently in only a handful of beta cities, and San Diego is not one of them.
- ▶ Neighborhood hosting, which has to do with helping your neighbors out when they get visitors in town.

People who are interested in Airbnb are looking for a different experience than what you typically receive in a hotel. I personally hate hotels and prefer to stay at an Airbnb. Think of two buddies going on vacation to a major city. I do this often with my buddy Travis. We each want our own room and this can cost a lot of money at a hotel. One place with two bedrooms and a kitchen makes sense. For a family of five, they would rather have one place to stay instead of separate hotel rooms to fit everyone in. Airbnb offers convenience and comfort.

Do I Lose Any Control Over My Property?

Absolutely not! Airbnb is a support platform that helps with marketing, some guidelines, and suggestions for you to have a successful experience. You control:

- ▶ The amount of space you'd like to rent out. This could be either a room, shared space, or an entire property.

- ▶ The rate you charge. Depending on where your property is, there are times when you may be able to receive a higher rate than others (more on this in marketing tips). I got almost one thousand dollars a night for three nights over Comic-Con weekend in San Diego.

- ▶ Who stays with you if you are doing a room rental in your home when you are there. There is an "instant booking" option on Airbnb and if you turn this feature on you are accepting anyone who wants to book.

- ▶ The dates you want to rent your property. You can block any dates you want for any reasons you want. Some people only want to book their place a couple of days a month and others want to book it 80 percent of the time.

- ▶ Any special conditions or stipulations you may have.

I have a friend who lives in the same city as his girlfriend, so he will look for weekends that he can get at least two hundred dollars a night for his place and then just sleep at his girlfriend's place over the weekend. This earns him a quick four hundred dollars for a weekend for basically doing nothing, because even the cleaning fee is paid by the guest.

What Does Airbnb Charge Me?

Currently, to take advantage of Airbnb's services, which include marketing, booking, and payment management, you will pay these fees:

- ▸ A 3 percent hosting fee after the guest is charged
- ▸ A 6 to 12 percent guest service fee that is charged to guests (dependent on property and conversion rates for foreign currency)

Is There Any Special Furniture I Need?

Remember, you are competing with hotels, which means you are best served to have some furniture. This is for creating the experience and for convenience of your guests. When you make sure to take good care of them you'll get better reviews. Reviews are important and will be covered later, but as a host everything you do should be targeted on one thing—establishing Superhost status. When you do this, you will increase your bookings and achieve first page status.

The rooms that you'll need to address if you're renting out an entire property are:

- ▸ **Bedroom:** Comfortable beds with two sets of good linens, pillows, and an alarm clock. I personally bought an eight hundred dollar king-sized bed on Amazon and people rave about it. Also, make sure there are plenty of blankets.
- ▸ **Bathroom:** Towels, soap, cleaning supplies, hair dryer.
- ▸ **Kitchen:** Utensils and dishes, coffee, tea, cleaning supplies.
- ▸ **Living room:** Seating is key, as well as a good TV and cable or dish provider.

- **Extras:** Pillows, blankets, good internet, toilet paper, paper towels, and so on.
- **Miscellaneous:** Great local attractions, specific bits of information that will make visitors' stays better. There will be a sample letter of what you can let guests know to make their experience better in the next chapter. This letter can also offer insights that protect you.

You'll also find an extensive list of information that is available when you take advantage of your free sign-up to become an Airbnb host on their site. You may be surprised, things you'd never think of—like never—are often important to others. It's important to remember that as an Airbnb host you are now in the hospitality industry, helping others have a great experience that you profit from. Depending on how much your guest is paying, you might want to leave them bottled waters, chocolates, a local souvenir, or even a bottle of champagne.

How Much of a Time Commitment Does it Take to Be an Airbnb Host?

Your set-up per property can take about forty minutes at first, a bit more or less depending on if it's your first listing or if you are a pro. After this initial set-up of a new property that is available, you'll want to be sure that you are designating the following time:

- Diligently answering inquiries and questions from potential guests or booked guests. You have twenty-four hours in theory to answer any questions, but with technology offering instant access I personally try to answer all questions within an hour. This will be known on your profile as your response rate.

▶ If you prefer, you can take a few minutes to meet your guests when they stay. This isn't always required or wanted, but offering it is a nice touch that will often add to your rating. Personally, I don't meet the people who stay with me and use the letter that they receive pre-arrival to lay everything out for them. Remember, this is optional and depends on how much time you have. Do you want to meet other people from different places in the United States and potentially the world?

▶ Booking the time to clean the property when the guest leaves. You can do this yourself and keep the cleaning fee, or if it works for you, factor in hiring a cleaning service into your bottom line. There are many services available that cater to the Airbnb model today that are worth taking advantage of, including management companies to handle all the details of your property. Note: it is required that you respond to all booked guest inquiries within twenty-four hours, which is sometimes only possible with the help of a management firm. The standard, accepted pricing for a property manager or management firm is 20 percent of the rental rate. This is all optional. For my properties, we do a pass-through cost with the cleaning fee, which means we charge the guest seventy-five dollars for a cleaning fee and that's how much I pay my cleaner. One time I stayed in Philadelphia and they charged a two hundred dollar-cleaning fee and the owner came and cleaned it. This was a quick two hundred dollars more in their pocket.

What are The Expenses that I Might Incur?

Airbnb is a business model and every business does come with expenses. You will definitely need to figure in:

- ▸ Mortgage expenses: principle, interest, taxes, and insurance.
- ▸ Utilities.
- ▸ Furnishings: I factor about four thousand dollars for a one-bedroom and eight thousand dollars for a two-bedroom in a large city.
- ▸ Amenities you feel may give you an "added value benefit," which may include basic food items (eggs, bread, milk, coffee, tea, and in my case, a few bottles of fine alcohol to enjoy if desired); games, gym passes.
- ▸ Taxes and tax liability.
- ▸ Toilet paper, paper towels, laundry detergent, fabric softener.

What If I am Not Located in the Same City as a Property I'd Like to Purchase?

I believe you need someone in the city to manage your properties if you don't live there or don't wish to be a hands-on manager. This could be a good friend, family member, or cleaning person you trust. This is important for emergencies or last-minute requests. Checking emails typically isn't a problem, as it's not location-specific; however, if someone is staying at your property and loses a key, you need responsiveness on a 24/7 basis for the entire time the unit is rented. Having someone who is responsive will make you receive better rankings. Additionally, finding a good maid that you can count on to thoroughly clean properties after they are vacated is a smart move. One of the biggest complaints you risk receiving is that the unit is not clean enough. Remember that as a host you are competing against hotels, so make sure that your unit is as clean as a hotel room is.

Tip: Use helpful technology

There are now keyless entries that you can put onto your units that work in conjunction with your smart phone. Give someone the access code, set the parameters for the time period when it is valid, and you avoid keys that don't work. Additionally, you can help circumvent any guests who are tempted to overextend their agreed upon rental period for your property. This gives you control, and you can determine when renters are coming and going from your property. I have not installed this in any of my units yet, but if I did not have a local person managing the unit I would, as it is a smart idea.

Does It Hurt Me to Not Make My Place Available for Rent All the Time?

In short—no. I have a place that I rent out in San Diego now, but as I'd shared earlier, I have to go to San Diego for up to two weeks a month, and when I do, I have my place blocked for the time when I want to stay at the unit. Overall, I seldom have over one or two days where my property is vacant. In the summer, the occupancy rate is about 95 percent and since I started the unit on Airbnb it has been a solid 82 percent, including the weekdays, which means it is rented for roughly twenty-four of the thirty days.

What's the Attitude About Neighbors and Others Nearby My Property?

Like most things in life, a little explanation up-front can nip the challenges that any neighbors who do not understand have. If you let them know that there are strict rules and expectations for your guests and that they will be there, most neighbors will be okay with that. Let them know that they are free to contact you—always. Once again, we send a list of rules with quiet hours and how to treat the property that we'll cover more intensely in a later chapter.

When you show your first interest is in being a good neighbor you'll save yourself time, hassles, and complaints. Reassure neighbors that you are doing things by the book and legally. Let them know its Airbnb so they aren't concerned. Additionally, Airbnb does have a tool for your neighbors called the Neighbor Complaint Tool, which can help you gain honest feedback to ensure you're keeping both your neighbors and guests happy.

How Do I Know Who Is Staying at My Property?

It makes sense that you want to know who is staying with you. As a protective measure against discrimination, Airbnb now has instant booking (a change from when it first began). However, every guest and host does have a profile that can be viewed by the other. This includes feedback that helps reassure you of the type of guest you may be receiving. It is very rare—despite the horror stories—that you'll have a guest who is a problem. They are there for an experience, not to trash your place, and this includes people there to party. Often, I will look up guests' LinkedIn profiles or see what they do for a living. Also, as a host you should always have a clear picture, smiling, where you look like a good, trustworthy person.

Is this legal?

Yes, Airbnb operates on a legal platform. Some cities such as New York and Santa Monica have banned short-term rentals, so I would check all the rules and laws of the city that you live in or wish to purchase investment property in. As mentioned, you are competing with hotels so you may not find hotel chains being huge fans of Airbnb, and even some cities where they rely on those big taxes from hotels to fuel their income. You'll have to do your due diligence and investigate:

- ▸ The guidelines in your city so you know what you can do with the Airbnb model to make it work for you.
- ▸ Your lease if you rent a property. These are considered short-term rentals and some leases prohibit these activities. How creative you want to get is up to you. There are accounts of individuals who start with a long-term lease and void it when a guest arrives, or go out of their way to ensure that any concerned parties are satisfied with what's happening so they don't run into trouble. A worst-case scenario is that you might have to pay your landlord or condo association the money you receive for a rental. It barely ever happens, but it pays to do your due diligence to see what your risk level may be.

How About Insurance for Short-Term Rental Use?

You should always have your standard insurance policies in place; however, Airbnb also has an insurance policy that provides a one million dollar-host guarantee. This won't cover personal possessions such as clothes, jewelry, cash on hand, and so on, but it will protect you from third-party claims such as injury or damage to your property by a guest. It is very important to realize what is not covered and to not leave around items you would be devastated to have stolen. I have very nice clothes and seven hundred belts and shoes that are often in my closet. In two years of hosting, I have never, ever had anything stolen. For the most part, people are responsible.

As you can see, those who have already begun to use the Airbnb model for their properties have made sure that many things are covered, and Airbnb has a very thorough model and policy guidelines in place. Just like you, they want this to be successful for as long as there's a place for it. The one thing to realize is that Airbnb does not own any properties. It is a platform provider so they need you just as much as you need them.

Future Forecast

The Deloitte Center for Industry Insights conducted research titled "Travel and Hospitality Outlook 2017" (www.deloitte. com/us/travel-hospitality-trends). Several factors were mentioned in this report, including those specific to the potential economic challenges for the industry, consumer expectations and demands, technology, and platforms. Here are some key takeaway points that are of interest regarding the increasing appeal of Airbnb:

- ▸ Global business travel became an over one billion dollar-a-year industry as of 2015, and is still rising.
- ▸ Being responsive to changes in the marketplace and what consumers want is an important indicator for success.

- U.S. leisure travel has grown at a rate of 5 percent for five consecutive years.
- The economy is in a growth and recovery period, which increases consumer confidence on several levels, including in the investing and travel industries.
- Airbnb has altered a consumer's definition of what a hotel is and what it should offer.
- Online travel agencies (Trivago, Trip Advisor, Expedia, and so on) continue to be a place where people go to plan their business and personal travel, both global and domestic. A strong online presence and platform are necessary in today's world.
- In striving for authenticity, Airbnb shows that there is a vast market for travel that lies outside the mainstream experience. Australia is the second biggest country in the world for Airbnb after the United States.

Growth is on the horizon, as evidenced by Airbnb turning its first profit in 2016, and estimates showing that revenue could topple 8.5 billion dollars by 2020. Uber, which has the biggest market capitalization of any company in the world, is not profitable and is still going through some major headaches right now, with key executives leaving daily. So, while Airbnb is similar to Uber in that they do not own the units, just a platform, the results are definitely not similar.

Do you want to be a part of this? That's what you must determine now. Not in 2020 after it all happens—now.

Evaluating Your Numbers

I'm a conservative investor, and with that comes a very methodical approach to determining what a wise investment is for me. I look at almost everything in life as a "reward versus risk" setup. Generally, the more risk you have, the more potential reward you should have as well. When it comes to real estate you have two primary ways to look at your investment and the money that you can make.

First is cash-on-cash returns. This type of return is determined by comparing the cash returned after all expenses, divided by the price for down payment, furniture for the unit, and cost of closing. Basically, this is the profit after all expenses divided by all capital from day one of purchasing the unit.

> When I look at possible investments I look at occupancy rate, average room rental, and so on. I try not to look at appreciation. As most investors who look at real estate look at cash-on-cash, I find ROI to be best for me, because I don't care what the cash-on-cash is as long as I'm putting money toward equity. Just like investing in stocks, you make money and you don't get it right away, you get it when you sell.

However, through evaluating a return-on-investment (ROI), you get some more insightful information. This evaluates the efficiency of an investment and may even compare the efficiency among a number of investments. This is a simpler, more versatile option, which makes it an appealing analytical tool.

The main difference between cash-on-cash and ROI is cash-on-cash return does not take into consideration the money paid on the mortgage toward the principal of the unit. Since it is going toward paying money toward equity, I find this very important. I do have a couple of units where my cash-on-cash return is 0 percent or very low, but since one thousand dollars a month is going toward building equity, I am getting closer to the 20 percent return.

The best way to determine what is best for you will depend on you—your preferences, comfort level, and ability to manage tax risks.

Cash-On-Cash Returns

The formula is simple, and it works regardless whether you purchase a property with financing or without. I highly recommend that you put at least the standard 20 percent down when purchasing; this will give you your best pricing, protections, and the ability to sell and likely make some money if the Airbnb model reaches its fullest potential and is no longer of interest to you.

Cash-On-Cash Returns Formula

$$\frac{\textit{Net operating income (NOI)}}{\textit{Total dollar investment}}$$

Investment properties often require 20 percent to 25 percent down payment. However, if it is your primary home you may only need 10 percent down, if that. Also, there are other loans that require 0 percent down (VA loans for example). The general rule is the less money that an investor has to put down the better the ROI and cash-on-cash return will be.

There are various expectations from all the professional real estate investors on what a healthy cash-on-cash return rate is. It ranges from 8 percent up to as high as 20 percent. I personally look for 15 percent if I'm looking at this number.

🏠 🏠 🏠

The following example includes all the factors that I feel are important in determining a cash-on-cash return calculation.

Note: I don't include maintenance, as most properties are a part of an association or complex that makes them low maintenance. If you are looking at assessments for a single-family property where this is not the case, a good number to factor in is 3 percent (if you don't want to use other funds to cover any potential costs). Also, including maintenance will impact your cash-on-cash return percentage.

Property Overview: Two-bedroom condominium in an urban setting

Expense	Cost
Property Purchase Price	$300,000
Mortgage Amount	$240,000
P&I Payment	$1,439.00 (assuming 6%)
Taxes, Insurance & Fees	$500.00
Utilities	$200.00
Monthly Property Cost	$2,139.00

Upfront Costs	Dollar Amount
Down payment (20%)	$60,000.00
Closing Costs	$2,000.00
Furnishing Property ($4K/bedroom/$3K living room/ $1K kitchen)	$8,000.00
Total Upfront Costs	$70,000.00

Target Average Rent	Rental/Day
21-day goal	$189.00*
Total Target Rent	$3,969.00

Airbnb Expense	Cost
Management Fee (On average, 20% of revenue, assuming 21 days booked)	$794.00 ($189 x 21 days x 20%)
Cleaning Fee** (Assumes 10 bookings for 2 nights)	$600.00
Airbnb Fee (3% in most cases)	$119.00
Total Average Expenses	$1,513

*We'll dive into it more with marketing tips, but you'll want to know the happenings in your Airbnb rental city. Conventions, celebrations, and "big draw" events can lead to higher rental prices during these times.

**On average, it takes three hours, assuming twenty-five dollars an hour to clean a two-bedroom condo.

To evaluate these numbers for cash-on-cash returns, you use a pretax cash flow to help determine the total investment. In this scenario, you are receiving a cash-on-cash return of about 5.4 percent. This may seem low, but you have to look at a larger picture to really understand the value of this strategy. You're putting money toward your principle, which is also an investment.

As far as the funds you invested up-front, if you'd held those same funds in an account for even ten years with an interest rate of 2.5 percent (a conservative choice) and with inflation that rate is actually closer to zero, you'd actually be losing money, because inflation is higher than that.

Additionally, the following is not even taken into consideration yet:

- ▸ Tax write-offs
- ▸ Depreciation write-off
- ▸ Increasing property values (appreciation)

We have already looked at appreciation being a big factor, but this is something I look as a bonus. I want to make money from the rental and not have to worry about appreciation. I think that if an investor is too concerned about appreciation they are missing the big picture. Also, I often will invest in a property that has lower cash-on-cash return or ROI if I know the potential appreciation is much higher. I mean, do you think that a property will appreciate more in value in San Diego or Boise, Idaho? My point exactly.

All these factors matter. Additionally, while I'd never say you shouldn't invest in the stock market—obviously—Airbnb shows an option that's outside of it, but can grow positively as the economy grows. On the flip side, if things start heading south, your investment isn't going to be flipped on its ear. This is about taking money and making it grow. I would like to get to the point soon where I just invest wisely in real estate and get checks in the mail.

Return-on-Investment Assessments

This formula terms "gain from investment" as the proceeds that could be obtained from the same of the investment. This makes it easier to compare an investment against other investments for performance measures. In theory, this is a simpler way for investors to determine an expected level of performance against many investment options. Many investors do not like this equation, but since it is building equity, I think this is a much better equation.

Return-On-Investment Formula

$$\frac{Gain\ from\ investment - Cost\ of\ investment}{Cost\ of\ investment}$$

Initial Investment	Costs
Property	$300,000.00
Total	$300,000.00

Sale of Investment	Incoming Funds
Property (Assumption: owned 1 year)	$320,000.00 (Assumption: 6.6% appreciation)
Total	$320,000.00

Difference	ROI
$20,000.00	6.6%

As you can see, this formula is simple; however, it doesn't take into account the whole investment picture.

Another way that people gauge the cost of an investment is even simpler. They use this basic formula:

Money received – money output per month = monthly profit plus principal paid

If you were to take this simple comparison, using the numbers listed for the sample property, you'd be looking at these estimated monthly earnings:

Target Earnings from Rental	$3,969.00
Minus Expenses	
P&I Payment	$(1,439.00)
Taxes, Insurance & Fees	$(500.00)
Utilities	$(200.00)
Management Fee	$(794.00)
Cleaning Fee	$(600.00)
Airbnb Fee	$(119.00)
Estimated Monthly Income	$317.00

If the principal is one thousand dollars, then the ROI would factor this in and I am really making one thousand dollars plus the 317 dollars a month—or 1,317 dollars a month. I would take that number, multiple by twelve, and divide that into the initial investment for my ROI.

As you decide whether to take advantage of today's Airbnb opportunity, this method is also going to allow you to compare this investment against other ones you may make, including those in a traditional stock market setting and bonds. I would say in this day of investing that with a riskless investment, 5 percent is good, 10 percent is great, and 15 percent is insane. If the ROI is above 30 percent I would be very skeptical of the property; it is probably a scam.

However, as a word of caution, you really are not comparing two similar things, and you'll also want to factor in your age. Are you at a point where you should be using more conservative strategies because you're nearing retirement? The general rule is that a person should have 100 percent minus their age in stocks and the rest in bonds. So, if you are thirty, you should be investing 30 percent in bonds and 70 percent in stocks. This is because as you get older, you need safer investments compared to when you are younger and can afford more risk. Airbnb is a part of the portfolio of my assets that I want to be riskier with. I am so confident that I want to put 35 percent of my net worth into it.

One of the major problems with the statement above is that the stock market is trading at all-time highs and if you factor in inflation of 2.5% then bonds give you zero return. That is not as bad as having money in your bank, because with inflation that will give you a negative return on your investment.

Perhaps you are more conservative by nature or simply do not feel you have bigger amounts of money to expose to high risk. If this is the case, Airbnb is a logical answer.

Tips and Formulas to Evaluate Your Income Potential

There are many resources online that can help you weigh what you are looking at regarding a return on your investment that works for you. Take advantage of:

▸ Tax information offered by your CPA
▸ Browsing Airbnb's listings and taking advantage of their rental pricing tools

Generalizing income is not easy to do and there is no guarantee with investments, even the highly appealing ones. This is why every single investment, Airbnb and otherwise, needs to be looked at with the "risk versus reward" setup. This is how I do all my trading, as well.

The decisions that can help guide you to knowing approximately how much you can make are mostly determined by:

▸ The market for your type of rental
▸ Your property location
▸ How you handle the expenses that are important in creating a marketable property for you
▸ The types of financing terms you are eligible for, specifically specialty loan programs and primary home loans

This is a lot to take into consideration, especially if you are diving into real estate investing for the first time. The great news is that you're now learning the basics and when you find a property, you'll have the understanding you need to make a smarter decision based on what the numbers and area you're looking in tell you.

I tell my subscribers the same thing I'm sharing with you: the stock market and trading should not be about emotions.

It is simply probability and math, and investing in anything should be the exact same thing.

The data on all this is available everywhere, because so many people are very interested. If you want to know more, just Google "Airbnb statistics" and you'll see that there are 596,000-plus results.

The best way to more easily grasp what you need to remember is by using an acronym that I use for all my properties. It is very simple to memorize and understand. That's right, just like ROY G BIV helps you remember the colors of the rainbow and Please Entertain Daddy And Sally helps you remember math, there are also key letters that create the formulas that help you know if you're investing strategically. For Airbnb learn these abbreviations:

O—Occupancy Rate: Average number of days unit is rented per month divided by the days in a month. Remember, many cities like Chicago and Phoenix will be seasonal; that's why I want the average through the year (expressed as a percentage). I usually want to be above 80 percent for any Airbnb.

A—Average Room Rate: Average price received per night throughout the year. This is going to average per month and you can calculate every month separately. For example, in Chicago you might get 249 dollars a night in July, but you might only get 99 dollars in December because some cities are more seasonal.

M—Mortgage: How much you have to pay for insurance, taxes, principal, and interest. Remember, some of these could be used as a write-off.

C—Cash-On-Cash Return: How much money will be received in profits divided by how much cash was outlaid (expressed as a percentage). Zero percent is fine since you are constantly paying money toward principal and building equity.

R—Return-On-Investment: I count money toward principal as ROI because it is building equity even though I won't see it until the property is sold or paid off. I strive to be at least 15 percent here.

T—Total Expense: This includes miscellaneous items such as supplies for the unit, repairs, and total mortgage.

S—Total Spent for Unit Until Rental-Ready: This includes everything you invest in a unit to prepare it for listing on Airbnb, and then receive your first booking.

P—Principal: Amount of money that goes toward paying down on a unit.

U—Sale Price of a Unit: How much a unit sells for.

V—Value Rise: How much it is believed that a property will appreciate per year (as a dollar amount). This is a hidden gem and often I do not factor this in just in case the real estate market starts to dip.

Through all these acronyms, just about everything you need to understand about a property and what it is costing you and earning you can be discovered.

Oscar **A**nd **M**ax **C**reate **R**eally **T**asty **S**trawberry **P**astries **U**sing **V**anilla

Here are a few samples of how I use formulas based on the acronym above. I take into account that more risk often leads to more reward, particularly if the price of a unit fluctuates throughout the year.

The OATSP System

This is the formula you would use for purchasing a unit with an R above 15 percent:

$$\frac{(O * A - T) *12}{(S + P)}$$

For example, I rent out a unit at an 80 percent occupancy for an average rate minus three thousand dollars a month for my expenses and mortgage.

Let's say I put up eight thousand dollars for furniture plus a down payment of one hundred thousand dollars. It would look like this:

$$\frac{(80\% * 30 * \$200) - \$3,000 *12}{(\$8,000 + \$100,000)}$$

$$\frac{(\$4800 - \$3600) * 12}{(\$108,000)}$$

Or 11.1 percent on cash-on-cash. Not too shabby.

This is the formula for buying a unit, with equity, with an R above 15 percent:

$$\frac{(O * A - T) *12 + V \text{ (the added gravy)}}{(S + P)}$$

Let's say I expect that place to go up 5 percent, which is rather low in real estate.

$$\frac{(80\% * 30 * 200 - \$3,000) * 12 + \$25,000}{(\$8,000 + \$100,000)}$$

$$\frac{(\$14,400 + \$25,000)}{(\$108,000)}$$

Or 36.4 percent. Now this is some great return.

The TOA System

This is the formula you use if you are not including the equity in a unit. It'll help you determine if it's still a good risk load that you're willing to take on. You always want your C to be above zero or you are losing money on a monthly basis. Use this formula to calculate it.

$$T - (O * A) = The\ TOA\ System$$
$$(80\% * 30* \$200) - \$3,000 = \$1,800\ a\ month\ of\ profits$$

Remember this: In some areas it is okay to have a unit at a negative C if one expects other months to crush it. These are more seasonal locations such as Chicago, Arizona, and so on.

In the end, I know how my formulas work for me and how to interpret the trends. It is always best for an investor to learn and memorize these formulas, but you also need to talk with your trusted tax professional to know how to best manage your finances. Taking all these steps is part of smart, informed investing.

And Taxes You Shall Pay

Knowing the right tax forms to file for your business will determine the amount of taxes you may owe, as well as the expenses that you will get to write off. You'll use either a Schedule E or a Schedule C, depending on how you choose to run your business.

- ▸ A Schedule E is used for passive income. This means that if you rent out a property and receive income from that rental, nothing more, this is the form that will work for you.
- ▸ A Schedule C is better suited to the Airbnb host who is providing more than just a space (experience hosts,

for example). You have the ability for higher deductions. The amount is dependent on your income and exact write-offs.

There are certain expenses that can be deducted for Airbnb if the property is not deemed a personal residence. A personal residence is defined as a place that you live in for over fifteen days of the month. It bears repeating—every individual case is different and you should talk to a tax CPA about this, not rely solely on me. This is a formula I call CYA.

If your property is deemed as an investment property you can take advantage of deductions such as: Airbnb commission, food and beverage costs you supply, cleaning and management fees, laptop and cell phone usage related to your business expenses, utilities, and any association dues related to your property.

Simplification Tip:
To keep all your Airbnb expenses separated from your other expenses you will want to establish a separate account for the property.

Being an Airbnb Host

"I really admire Airbnb as a pioneer of the sharing economy and for building community. They've found an elegant way to help hosts make more money and for guests to have authentic experiences. It brings those people together in a unique way."

— LOGAN GREEN, CEO OF LYFT —

You've researched it. You're ready. It's time to put it all into play and list your property so you can eventually become a host. Consider yourself "Host Official," because you are a step closer to getting your first booking.

The listing is one of the most important aspects to consider for your Airbnb property if you want to make money. I have often changed my ad multiple times to make the unit get more listings and thus make me more money.

Before we get too far, let's start with a brief lecture, albeit a necessary one. If a potential guest asks you to work with them outside of Airbnb to pay lesser fees, as tempting as it may be, say "no." Never, ever do this. You wouldn't have made the connection without Airbnb for starters, but additionally, Airbnb offers a highly valuable platform for investors to make money. Everyone wins and it is more secure. If that doesn't sell you on how serious I am about this, think of the flip side. You own Airbnb and people use your technology and resources to make money, but insult you by skirting paying you. Ouch. Plus, it's against their policy and if you break it, you can say goodbye to the golden platform. It won't be an option for you any longer. Airbnb has been known to kick hosts off the platform because of this. Your unit is also not going to be protected by the insurance policy if you go outside of Airbnb. Why risk it?

🏠 🏠 🏠

To be the ultimate host on Airbnb you have to operate on an ethical level and delve into the full scope of what this means. I personally always believe that honesty is the best policy and I feel this begins with the listing. Even if your listing is not the best, do not make it seem that it is something that it is not. It will kill your ratings and lower your chances of making money.

In this chapter, you're going to have a lot of information thrown at you. A lot of it you can learn before you even begin—an advantage that the first wave of Airbnb investors did not have. However, a bit of it will come with time and experience. If you're committed and focused on your business and how you can grow it, you'll be able to manage all of it.

Property Considerations

At this point you either have a property that you'd like to put onto the Airbnb platform, or you are going to seek a property that you'd like to purchase for use as an Airbnb rental.

If you currently own the property you need to evaluate its strengths and weaknesses, in comparison to what potential guests look for. With every unit I buy I like to add some local flavor and make my guests feel like they are gaining some culture. In San Diego, I always have quotes about the ocean and beach because I know even if someone is on business they will likely head to the beach for some relaxation.

1. **Location:** depending on your city and the type of property you have, you will want to either emphasize how great your location is or offer information to guests that shows them that in your case "off the beaten path" equates to a hidden gem. Taking advantage of the stats and data on location for your city can help you make the best decisions.

   Every unit will appeal to different end-users. I actually try to appeal to all users: a) the partygoer; b) the family; and c) the businessperson. For the partygoer, I want them to know that my units are close to all bars/restaurants. For the family I want them to know my place is very quiet and not a lot of noise. For the businessperson, I always let them I have a nice clean desk, chair, fast internet, and am very near a convention center.

2. **Type of rental:** if you're going to be renting out a room or the goal is to share a single room, you'll want to clearly define what your interaction will be with a guest and what is offered as a part of that deal.

   Note: 29 percent of listings are for a single room offering and 2 percent of listings are for sharing a room; the remainder is for an entire home/apartment. Anyone in the world can make extra money for any of these three separate categories, but all my units are whole units.

3. **Type of property:** the biggest area where you'll have to make considerations here is if you are listing a condo or a property that you currently rent. You'll have three choices, and only you can determine which one fits best for you.

   Choice #1: Ask for permission if it's against the regulations and policies of the Home Owners Association (HOA) for short-term rentals. Exceptions can be granted, but if they are not, be prepared because this may impact you if you're renting out more than a room in your primary residence. Before investing in a property, please read the HOA rules and regulations. The last thing someone who wants to purchase a property for Airbnb rental wants is to find out after the fact that the board will not make exceptions.

   Choice #2: List the property without permission. With this step, I recommend being on good terms with neighbors and letting them know you have a lot of friends that stay with you. Give them your number and let them know you are definitely concerned with them not having bad experiences in their homes due to your guests. I feel it's also important to disclose that if your HOA finds out about this, they could have a rightful claim on all rents you received without their approval. Also consider the ramifications of getting busted, which could lead to eviction. Being evicted creates challenges for finding a new place to live. I have heard many horror stories about huge fines of over one hundred thousand dollars and being evicted in the building. The board and the majority of unit holders control the HOA. One great way to control the rules of the HOA and control the board is to either get on the board or purchase multiple units in the same building so you have more say.

Choice #3: Decide against listing on Airbnb. Obviously, if this choice is what you'd do, the rest of this information doesn't mean too much, does it?

A few selling points you could consider when trying to get an exception for you to list your property on Airbnb are wise to have in your pocket. The following list includes what I feel are the strongest, most compelling points.

1. **Find a compromise.**
   If it's a rental property or an association property, many times there can be compensation given for the exception to rent out a room or property. Perhaps a slight increase in your rent, or a percentage of income paid (10 percent up to 30 percent is standard) for your exception. Think like a deal maker and you may stand a chance. I have never done this before and I always look for units that are stand-alone units, which means that there is no board and they are HOA-friendly.

2. **Share what Airbnb really offers.**
   You understand a great deal by this point, and you can let landlords and HOAs understand that when you are an Airbnb host you are held accountable. You get rated and reviewed based on the quality of the property and the experience someone has when they are staying there. If anything, you are the hassle-free tenant, especially if you have a meaningful discussion with neighbors about your guests, reiterating to your neighbors that your guests understand their needs.

3. **Achieve Superhost status first.**

   This is for the person who is interested in more than one investment on the Airbnb platform. However, it's a powerful idea because you can lend evidence to back up your claim with feedback, great ratings, and an obviously preferred status on the platform that homes many millions of hosts. Superhosts are hard to achieve, but once an investor becomes one they will see their listing rent more and can charge a higher price. Why wouldn't Airbnb want to reward a host who is a good host, who has a clean unit and great ratings? People are visual, as evidenced by how a listing should be completed, and if you can hand over visual proof of how important taking good care of your rental property is you increase your negotiating power. Furthermore, the person you have to address regarding the subject of an Airbnb rental can verify all this online. By doing this, you'll be able to literally show them the evidence.

4. **Have strict house rules.**

   One of the smartest and most strategic moves that Airbnb has made is allowing the host to operate like a small business owner. You have certain laws and guidelines you must follow, but overall you can set your own rules and fees for everything. This means that you can have the house rules that a guest must have right on the listing, or ask them to request a copy of them. This can save you from getting into sticky situations if someone ignores the rules. Likewise, it will stop most guests from booking in a place where they know they don't have a chance of adhering to the rules you've set. For example, smokers aren't going to rent a place that doesn't allow smoking. We also tell our guests that they are not allowed to have parties and there are quiet hours. For the most part, guests are considerate and will listen to the rules.

5. **Establish your target market.**
Knowing to which guests you would like to rent can help alleviate problems. We have identified the three main renters: partygoers, family and business travelers. I actually try to make my unit great for every single category. Just be mindful that you cannot discriminate, as this was an initial, unintentional problem with Airbnb. However, you do have the right to appeal to just business travelers, family vacationers, or party people if that's what you prefer.

The overall message: you'll never know unless you ask.

The Right Rate

"Price is what you pay. Value is what you get."
WARREN BUFFET

Getting the price that is average for your property, or even a bit higher price, all comes down to what type of property you have, its location, and how you market it. You wouldn't think it is important to market it, but approaching marketing like this is a small business is important. So is keeping an eye on all your expenses.

The most basic way to determine if you can make a profit is to take your Revenue (R) and subtract your Total Costs (TC).

As with any property, there are some costs that you can easily determine because they are fixed. These costs include:

- ▶ Mortgage
- ▶ TV/internet
- ▶ Insurance
- ▶ Local taxes
- ▶ Cleaning
- ▶ Routine maintenance

Other costs cannot be so easily pinpointed. They depend on utility usage, emergency situations, and unanticipated costs. These are termed marginal costs and include:

- ▶ Gas and electric
- ▶ Water
- ▶ Misc. supplies
- ▶ Management costs
- ▶ Nonstandard maintenance

Assume that your fixed costs come to two thousand dollars per month for your property and your marginal costs approach eight hundred dollars per month. When this breaks down it comes to:

Fixed Costs (assuming a 30-day month)
$67.00 per day
Marginal Costs (assuming a 30-day month)
$27.00 per day

Basically, you are paying ninety-four dollars per day to live at your residence. If you are either tight on cash or interested in generating more income you can rent out a room for even fifty dollars a day and offset this number by a fair amount.

It makes sense. Also remember that no matter how great the property is or how well you market it, you will almost never be at 100 percent occupancy; 80 percent is a great number to aim for.

Or, if the property is vacant and you've tried traditional renting, you definitely know that any activity is better than no activity for your bottom line. Remember that you must also be accountable for some essentials, as you cannot rent out a place that does not have any furniture at all. You need a king/queen bed for every two people you are hosting, towels, sheets, blankets, basic kitchen supplies, a couch, internet, and electricity, let's not forget that. It is possible to rent a unit without TV and cable, but be honest with the renter on the description. Most likely no one will rent it without internet, making that a must.

The bottom line is that if you can get more money for a single day for your property than what your marginal cost is, renting it out is profitable.

At this point you are not making money, but you are doing two strategic investment moves:

1. Offsetting expenses
2. Establishing a solid Airbnb reputation

It's your lucky day and you've rented your place out for forty-seven dollars per day. You're making twenty dollars a day, and that's nice, but not quite nice enough. What you do next is determine which profit margin makes the most sense to you. Let's say you decide that renting the property for sixty-seven dollars per day will work well for you because you can live with a forty dollar-per-day offset. This is a great deal for a single guest.

Now, what if you want to cater to multiple guests at once (which you should unless it's a private room rental in your home)? What you do next is dive into your potential guests' minds. Think about how much they'd pay for a hotel if there were two, four, or even six of them. They'd likely be looking at two bedrooms or a suite—average price of two hundred dollars per night or way more, dependent upon city and personal preference. If you set a rate for the property of 147 dollars per night, you are suddenly looking at a good net profit of approximately fifty-three dollars per day (based on paying ninety-four dollars per day average for your place).

This sounds pretty good, which means that it is time to see how your property compares to others on Airbnb that are similar and in your location. Remember, the two main competitions for your units are hotels and other Airbnb units in a similar location.

- ▶ If you're in the ballpark, you have your price.
- ▶ Or, if you're lower than others you know you can adjust upward a bit and be good. (*Tip:* it's not a horrible idea to start out low just to get some ratings at first. After that you can price correctly.) At the beginning of any listing, you will need to keep your rates at about 80 to 85 percent of the going rate. This is to attract buyers; but once you get ratings you can take prices higher. Also, once you become a Superhost you can actually charge more than other hosts. Remember that Rome was not built in a day, so take your time and be patient.
- ▶ And maybe you're overpriced, which takes you back to what is acceptable for you or not.

It's rare that you won't be able to find a sweet spot that satisfies you, the host, and your target guest market. If you are at 80 percent booking for two months out your price is probably too low, but if you are at 30 percent occupancy rate then your prices are probably too high.

You can also take advantage of certain pricing tools if you want some technology to do the work for you. It's not a bad idea to compare a number you come up with against what they say, just to confirm or let you know that you need to reevaluate.

With the pricing services available, some are better than others. This is completely individual preference. There are two main options, but many vendors are available for third-party pricing (check out resources in the back of the book).

1. **The Airbnb pricing calculator:** this helps you determine which rates to charge at certain times. This may be dependent upon day of the week, time of year, length of time out for the booking, or any other indicators that can impact how much or little you might charge to have the best chance of occupancy. I have never used this before and I do not believe that this is a good source from what I have read. I would rather see what my competitors in my area are charging; this may take a little more time, but a little more time could mean a lot more money.

   Blue indicates Airbnb's pricing recommendation—go below this and you'll likely receive a booking.

   Orange indicates that your pricing is above the Airbnb recommend "tip" and your chances of receiving a booking decrease. But hey, you're the boss and business owner, it's your call. This is very similar to *Shark Tank*. As a business owner would you rather want 50 percent of a one million dollar-company or 100 percent of a 250,000-dollar company? This again is just a mathematical equation and it's a game. I love games so I love trying to get the most amount of money from my guests.

Airbnb stands strongly by its pricing calculator for obvious reasons, but you want to compare it against others. Do not just assume that your profits will be maximized with it, as this is not always the case.

Ather benefit that is nice about taking advantage of the resources that Airbnb uses is that you can gain access to new testing tools that they offer. They are always striving to make everyone's experience better, and for hosts this includes profits. From where I stand today, I believe they will improve on their pricing tool feature; however, I choose to pass on it at this time.

2. **Third-party pricing:** the services that can automatically read the market, going rates, and automatically update you to when you may want to consider adjusting your pricing are wonderful resources. They work in real time, which is invaluable, because potential guests can be looking at your property 24/7.

   The way these third parties determine your suggested rental rate include evaluation of:

   ▶ Visitor stats
   ▶ Occupancy rates for comparable listings
   ▶ The current costs of airline seats
   ▶ Pricing for hotel bookings in the area

If you can easily leave something to automation's care once you've established it, this is a great option for you because you quite literally don't have to think about it. However, if you're like me, you love numbers and trends and want to absorb as much as you can from all that data. You pay attention.

Overall, with the right set rate that is also a marketable rate you can accelerate your rise to becoming an elite Airbnb investor and host more quickly like myself.

Pricing Flexibility

You never look a gift horse in the mouth, or so I've heard. Personally, I've never had the chance. However, I know that you should always appreciate and perhaps salivate over the chance to create a long-term guest or a repeat guest. One of my units has the same person renting it for Comic-Con in San Diego every year, where I can charge almost one thousand dollars a night for three nights. To offer perspective, this is five times the going rate. I don't even have to worry about renting the unit because this repeat guest always wants it.

In sales, it has long been noted that it's hardest to get a client for the first time. Once you take great care of them, they will want to come back. This definitely works with the Airbnb model. Also, other people will be more inclined to purchase a product if they know that other people have bought it already.

A few areas that you may want to exercise flexibility in include:

1. Guests who will be there for a longer period, even if it's a week or a month. Perhaps offer them a 10 percent to 20 percent discount for this. It is easier to manage four guests in a month than fifteen, because of checking in, checking out, cleaning with the maid, and so on. We have looked at the kind of returns. Heck, I would much rather have one person stay there all month and then it is set it and something I don't have to address. Decide if you'd like to extend this right away or if you would like to offer it to them for a future stay.

2. Use the infamous, time-tested, and seen everywhere sales approach of having "digit pricing." This is the pricing you see everywhere, in which the price may

end in either .97 or .99. If you have a rental price of 149.99 dollars it's suddenly more appealing than 150 dollars. I use all these pricing strategies with my internet marketing products and it works great. Admit it, you've probably fallen into this psychology in your life. What makes it more interesting is that people will often round down. Say you ask someone how much he or she paid for something. They'll say 149.99 instead of 150 dollars. Strange to think how a single penny could cost you an entire booking, but it has been proven that it can.

3. Negotiate your rate. If you're comfortable with this, it's a great way for a host and a guest to both feel like they've won. If you do it in a friendly way you are also developing some sound rapport that will help when it comes to reviews. I have even gotten to the point that when I travel I try to get a lower price than the listing price. I mean, a hotel will not do this for advanced bookings and who wants to wait until you need a place to stay to try. However, with an Airbnb host it never hurts to ask as a guest. This is another hidden gem I am sharing with you in this book, it helped me saved over $300 on my last trip to Mexico. This could save you a ton of money in the long run. Just make sure you tell them not to include that you negotiate in their review, because you really don't want to have to negotiate every deal. It should be the exception to your bookings.

4. Extra charges are something you may want to consider. In specific, extra guests and cleaning can warrant these charges. For example:

- ▶ If they want five people to stay in your four-person property, you could charge an extra twenty-five dollars per night. We do this, because we know that the extra person will mean extra cleaning and utility costs.

- ▶ Consider having a cleaning fee for your listing. It hasn't shown that it impacts booking rates and it can be a great way to offset costs for either a larger party or a long-term rental. Some people will go less on the rent to charge this. It evens out in the end, but it's perception. We do a pass-through charge. This means whatever we pay for cleaning is what we will charge the guest. There are many people who charge more and try to profit that money, but I feel it is unethical so I do not do it.

- ▶ If your property is considered high end or is unique in some manner, you can consider charging a security deposit. Remember, there is no guarantee on the Airbnb insurance policy for jewelry, cash, art, and watches. The guest isn't charged it unless there's damage you can prove, and it gives you reassurance if you feel it's necessary. This has been known to give many people horror stories. I look at it like this: if it breaks is it a big deal? And if the answer is yes then I will not keep it in my unit.

Flexibility can help you gain more bookings and still make money. No matter what you decide to do and when, you'll want to go with what instinctually feels right to you.

Account Establishment and a Golden Listing

To get started as a host you'll visit the Airbnb.com home page and create an account if you do not have one. There's a button in the upper right corner that reads "Sign Up."

Choose the option you'd like to use to sign up.

1. Use either Google, Facebook, or email to sign up.
2. Come up with a secure password. I always forget my password, but it's easy to reset it if you are always losing it like me.
3. Enter your address, telephone number, and other information that you're prompted to answer.
4. Put your picture on your profile. More details on this are shared further in the chapter.

For your online safety, they will have a two-factor authentication process, which will verify that it's really you. This can be sent to your phone or email—your preference.

From here, select the "List Your Space" option in the top right corner. This will take you to a prompt to enter all the details of your property.

Next, it's time to do everything that will make your property listing be complete—and if you do it right, amazing! We will give you all the tips and tricks that you need to make your listing great.

The best listings have mastered some key components that make them pop. They make the difference between an amateur and a professional. And absolutely, without a doubt, they make a difference between a booked property and a vacant property. Once again, I cannot tell you how important it is to think of your Airbnb listing as a small business. Do you want to be the best business owner or are you being lazy and missing some key steps?

I don't want you to feel you can skimp on any area of your Airbnb hosting, but a good listing is absolutely necessary. Without it, your listing will be lucky to be found at all, unless the person starts from the bottom up. Really, who does that? And imagine if you live in Paris. Not good! They have forty thousand-plus property listings there. Paris is the city that has the most Airbnb listings of any in the world, just in case you wanted to know.

You'll want to carefully address the following seventeen areas to increase your chances of having the most compelling listing available.

1. **Type of rental**
   Nobody wants to be shocked and learn that they are the "plus one" during their rental time. Many times—more often in Europe—the host does not disclose how many people are staying in "one unit" as long as they are advertising it as a "private room." However, I think this is unethical and would never do this. Clearly define if you're renting an entire home or apartment (which comprises 69 percent of all listings), a private room, or a shared room and be up-front and honest about it.

2. **Overview of property**
   This is 250 words and a title that give people a basic insight into your property. The title should never say the city name, which is a simple rookie mistake that we know you make now. Also, in the description I try to attract all three of the possible guests that we talked about. Here's an example:

   Quiet (for family) Luxurious Business Friendly Condo Close to Bars and Restaurants

All potential buyers for my property have been attracted through this type of title. The way it is worded is a natural sales draw.

On the screen, you will fill the information in for a potential guest to review. You'll see buttons for editing and inputting the data.

3. **Pictures**

If you are in a city that has it, take advantage of the professional picture services of Airbnb. You will not regret it. In fact, you might profit from it. It is free; why would you not take advantage of this?

Professional pictures can help you earn up to an estimated 2.5 times more money than amateur images. You have to have an eye for photography and all the nuances that go along with it, which include:

- ▶ Lighting (early morning and late afternoon are considered best)
- ▶ Staging (a picture-perfect room). The key to staging is to make the possible guest picture it as if they were there. This could include putting a coffee mug or Apple computer in the pictures.
- ▶ Best angles
- ▶ Most appealing images
- ▶ Determining which photograph is your "attention grabber" – your leader
- ▶ Interesting features that may help to sell, such as a gourmet kitchen, high-speed internet, a stellar sound system, or an outside view that is killer amazing. You want to take pictures of what makes your property unique and/or why your place is better than the other one hundred listings in that city.

You'll want to use images for a property that make it distinct and appealing to consumers.

For starters, there is the header picture, which is the first one everyone will see. The property is titled "Penthouse with BEST Views and Rooftop Pool & Gym."

The interior photos should be friendly and inviting and show why it is such a popular rental choice.

4. **Profile**

   Your profile is going to be important to people viewing your property because they are placing a great deal of trust in you, just as you are in them. You want to represent yourself impressively and be honest. In general, people are more likely to trust others who are in pictures with animals, a significant other, and smiling. I recommend taking advantage of the thirty-second video that Airbnb allows you to post where you can share a message with potential guests. This also serves as a great tool for creating that connection that helps when it comes to reviews. If someone trusts you they will most likely be willing to give you a better review and, in turn, you will trust them more.

5. **Personal photograph**

   You don't need to have a headshot like you might for a traditional business card or your business's website page. It can be a bit more casual. However—and this is not optional—you need to make sure the image is:
   - ▶ Clear and of high quality (high resolution)
   - ▶ Friendly—sport a smile
   - ▶ You can clearly see your face and eyes
   - ▶ Your dress isn't too casual. An example for women is having too much cleavage showing.

For the guys, take a pass on the muscle shirts. Remember, this isn't Instagram and you are not trying to pick up girls; leave the shirtless selfies on social media. Business casual is ideal.

▶ Your personal hygiene is in order. Looking disheveled equates to looking frazzled and out of control.

6. **Your Airbnb symbol**

If you love creativity this is the ideal chance to infuse a little you into your listings. And even if you don't love creativity, Airbnb has you covered with their symbol maker. You can create this and it will be a personal signature mark of your listings. This is only just an added touch, but it is important to consider anything that can possibly get you the listing or to stand out among others. It's all about your potential revenues and profits.

7. **Title**

The title is a draw, and should be created based on your primary audience. If you want to attract business clients you may want to consider a title such as this: Quiet Urban Setting with Modern Business Amenities. Be descriptive with words that are appealing and marketable. A few such words include: luxurious, urban setting, perfect location, and so on. Being mindful about what I've already shared about making your property appealing to multiple people is important here. As mentioned, I don't just want to appeal to one traveler, but all types. Whatever you decide on, make sure the title addresses these components:

▶ Grab the users' attention with appealing, visual words

▶ Provide key information regarding the type of space you are renting

Additionally, you can change titles as necessary if special events are coming to town. When Comic-Con comes to town, let the masses of attendees know that they are welcome in your home. Remember that events like Comic-Con will get five times the revenue of a normal Saturday night. My rule of thumb is that if a special event does not attract two times the rate for any other night, I will not change the title just for that event.

8. **Description**
They love the pictures. They are intrigued by the title. Now they want to know more. This is where you describe exactly what you are offering and express it in such a way that they will either "heart" it to possibly book later, or just book right away. Imagine that you are single and talking to a girl at the bar. You want to tell her all your great qualities, not the bad ones. This is the same thing. Be sure to emphasize everything that makes your place great and use as many adjectives as possible. The must-have information for a description includes:

▶ Size of the property

▶ Number of bedrooms and bathrooms

▶ Outdoor area descriptions for balconies, decks, and so on. *Do not include public space if you are in a condo or apartment that has such amenities.*

▶ Room descriptions

- Depending on your preference and flexibility mention if you go out of your way to accommodate the guest. For example, we always have a blowup bed and a pullout couch; this way we can sleep six in a one-bedroom. Remember, that bachelor party just wants to pack as many people as possible for the cheapest price. We let potential guests know this.
- Maximum number of guests. We set a one-bedroom at six and a two-bedroom at eight unless they want to pay extra.
- Mention if the unit is ground level or upper level.
- Are there elevators on site?
- Parking availability. If you have a spot and are not using it this is a huge bonus, especially in big cities where overnight parking could cost anywhere between twenty-to-fifty dollars a night and is not convenient.
- Proximity of supermarkets, bars, or restaurants
- If your property is not in a family or pet-friendly area, you may want to mention this as well.

Additionally, do not be too vague or dull with your words. Do not write this:

The master bathroom has a clawfoot tub.

Boring, yawn.
Instead, try this:

After a long day enjoying the sights, indulge in the luxury of a bath in the clawfoot tub while sipping some local wine and eating cheese.

What a difference a description can make. Now the reader has pictured himself or herself having a wonderful experience in your property. If you don't feel you have the poetic gift to create an appealing description, you should hire a professional copywriter to help, or one of the Airbnb property description services. If you feel stuck it helps to use adjectives and imagine what you want out of a vacation listing. This is probably what your guest wants also. Relaxation, quiet, and possibly even romance.

Show what you offer without overselling or intentionally misleading guests. Never, ever mislead a guest and promise or tell them anything that is not true. I promise you if you do this, you will never get to Superhost status and you will never be on the front page when they search your city.

9. **Amenities**

   List everything that's included with your property, from washers and dryers through hairdryers, and so on. When I Airbnb'ed my first property I would never have imagined a hairdryer because I am a guy, but this is a must. Also, hangers, bottle and wine openers, iron, and ironing board. Just imagine the same things that are at a hotel.

10. **House rules**

    What you expect from your guests is important to set up-front. You can put this in your description. or to start a dialogue you can suggest they message you to get a copy of the rules. The upside to people seeing it right away is they may book right away. These rules should include quiet hours, smoking policies, parties, pets, extra guests policy, when doors lock, and so on. The last thing you want is to come home after a long weekend out of town and find your place trashed.

11. Minimum/maximum number of nights

Your minimum/maximum number is going to adjust as you establish your reputation on Airbnb. When you first start, you should not hesitate to have a one-night minimum and one-week maximum (in my opinion). The reason for this is that you want to establish reviews, learn how the complete process works, and determine if there are any improvements that should be done to your profile, description, special offerings, and so on. Now, I try not to do a listing for one night unless it is last-minute and I want to squeeze out another one hundred dollars; remember that coordinating with other guests coming in and getting the maid does require a little bit of time. Also, be careful of anyone who wants to stay more than thirty days. This is because there are squatter laws in some cities. Also, as we talked about before, never, ever book your place to anyone on a "side" deal.

12. Rush requests

When someone wants to rent your property quickly—as in the same day—you have a choice to say no, or to say yes and perhaps attach some stipulations to it. A few ideas that you could include:

- ▶ Tell them you need at least four hours advance time so you can put the hustle on to make sure you are giving them a fully prepared property and cleaned.
- ▶ Have an additional rush check-in fee. If they want to check-in within twenty-four hours of booking the property, this allows you to possibly pay someone a bonus to help you make this happen.

For my properties, whenever anyone wants to check in early or late, as long as it does not distract other guests' check-ins or the maid, we are always fine with it. It might also lead to a better review. Possibly they just want to drop off their bags, which I am fine with as well.

Ultimately, if the money is there and waiting to be paid to you, you don't live there, and you have the resources to make it happen, I say, "Why not do it?"

13. **Instant bookings**

This is a new feature and every single host can either have instant booking on their listing or not. Instant bookings make it so a guest doesn't have to begin any specific interaction with you to reserve your property. This can be convenient, but it can also be risky, especially if it's your primary residence. You have the option to set up parameters where guests who have no reviews cannot use instant booking. This gives you a chance to talk to them and learn a few things, such as: 1) Why are you visiting the area? 2) How many people will be staying with you? 3) What do you hope to do during your stay? 4) Do you have any questions on the house rules? We have opened our listing to instant bookings and knock on wood, we have not had any problems so far. However, it is riskier.

It's also important to mention that if you have instant bookings cancel more than three times per year, you're going to have a potential penalty associated with this. This stipulation adds another risk factor to instant booking, as compared to manual bookings.

14. Manual bookings

This is my preferred route, as I find it makes for a much better experience for everyone. You can take advantage of the "Discuss" option and begin a conversation where you get to know each other better and feel things out before you agree to let them stay. Remember this though—no discrimination is allowed. This has been a major problem with Airbnb and I do not tolerate it at all. I say, all the money is green, which means I would never, ever turn anyone down because of sex, race, or age.

15. Advanced bookings

How you operate this will depend on a few things, including if you live at the property when it's not being rented and the type of location you are at. As a standard, six months to a year out is fairly common for destinations that are big tourist/vacation attractions. The further out you are willing to list it, the better. I recently had someone book a listing five months out as I wrote this book. However, keep premium dates in mind, because this could be a source of even more money and you do not want to give away premium nights for standard price.

You can set the parameters for this on your listing page though. Before you do so, evaluate your own life if you live at the property. If someone wants to book out a year, is it a time that works for you? And, is it feasible for you to find another place to stay?

16. Cancellation policy

You have six options for this so you can't create your own custom plan. According to Airbnb policies you can either be:

Flexible: give a full refund for any cancellations that take place twenty-four hours prior to arrival. They even have a clock that helps cover what "twenty-four hours" means. If it's even a minute late, the guest will receive notice they are being charged for a day if they cancel. It gives them the chance to reconsider. Since all our listings are vacation spots, I do not like this option. If someone is locking down my listing and holding it so another person cannot book it, I feel it's important to be very strict with cancellations.

Moderate: offer a full refund for any booked guest who cancels within five days prior to their arrival. Again, the clock will help you relay the interpretation of this to the guest. Once again, this depends on location. We are above 80 percent occupied so if we give a cancellation it is taking money out of our pockets.

Strict: guests can cancel up to one week ahead of arrival for a 50 percent refund. This still can cost the host money so I do not think it is best.

Super strict thirty days: guests can receive a 50 percent refund if they cancel within thirty days of arrival time. From my point of view, this is very fair.

Super strict sixty days: guests can receive a 50 percent refund if they cancel within sixty days of arrival time. This might be a stretch but it all depends on you. This is your small business, how you want to run it is up to you.

Long-term: you would require the first month down payment, and a thirty-day notice before the lease could be terminated. Once again, I do not recommend any long-term rentals through Airbnb.

By no means should you let people take advantage of your lack of restrictions on your property, but many times this is what you have to do when you are beginning the Airbnb process. Is it absolutely necessary? No, but you should base your decisions on your property, personal comfort level, and whatever other criteria you may have that are pertinent and specific to you. After you have reached a target goal of occupancy—say 80 percent—you should be confident to switch to the Moderate policy.

17. Understand the Airbnb Host Guarantee

This is the insurance policy for up to one million dollars that I mentioned. It covers damage to a property and certain other events. However, it does not cover someone stealing your clothes, dishes, electronics, watches, jewelry, art, or cash. I remove anything that is too valuable. I do often leave my expensive belts and shoes in my properties, but I have never had a problem.

Make sure you understand what an eligible claim for this is. It's designed to help protect the most expensive asset you have invested in your business: your property. You'll want to check with your insurance provider to see if you need a special rider for protecting other assets for short-term rental situations. Just because Airbnb does offer an insurance policy doesn't mean you get a paid claim overnight. Think of a car claim or even a homeowner's claim; it is not like they write you a check overnight. It can take a long time.

Another idea would be to buy a safe that is bolted down if this is your primary home and it is a pain to consistently remove items from your unit.

All these considerations are what will help you prepare yourself to become a thriving host, and eventually a Superhost if you remain disciplined.

The Welcome Packet

You want to make you guests feel at home when they arrive, and part of that is welcoming them with a professional letter that shows how important their stay is to you. You can deliver this via email and/or text and usually within five days at most before they arrive.

A few things that you will want to provide information for in your welcome packet include:

- ▶ Passwords for Wi-Fi or entrances where one may be required. We also leave a sign inside any unit to make sure the guest knows the Wi-Fi—which is #1 for most guests, including me when I am one.
- ▶ A listing of local events going on that may be of interest.
- ▶ Restaurants and grocery stores that you recommend. This is always great information to get from a local who has lived in the area for a while.
- ▶ Some gifts and small memberships; I have a friend who owns a gym and is glad to comp passes for my guests' stay. I know from my travel experiences that this can often cost me twenty dollars a day, so this is always nice.
- ▶ House rules such as quiet hours, maximum guests, and so on.
- ▶ Any information that adds value to their stay. Putting together an Airbnb Guidebook through their website for guests is a great way to do this, as well. You could

even go as far and have extra welcome guides for the three major guests. I have a friend who always gets me buy one-get one free (BOGO) bottles at the night-clubs. Why not pass this on to my guest? This way, my friend is always willing to take care of me when I come to the club.

▸ An amazing letter that gives them a resource that tells them the messages you have for them. I email this and my property manager hands it to guests when they arrive.

To me, this welcome packet and letter is of the utmost importance, as it helps to ensure that both the guest and the host are on the same page with a great many topics, while letting my guests see that I am a host who is completely vested in their stay. I want it to be incredible so they talk about it...and come back.

Here's a sample of what the letter looks like:

Welcome to Sunny San Diego!

I'm excited to have you here as my guest and provide you everything you need to make your stay enjoyable. First, a few basic guidelines for your visit:

• If you follow the rules, neighbors won't be concerned with who you are, but if they ask, just tell them that you're visiting me. If they have questions they will send me a message. Mentioning Airbnb isn't necessary.

• If you have problems of any sort during your stay, you need to contact Cameron Stein via call or text. He is the one who can assist with all these needs and is available 24/7. His number is 999.999.9999 and his email is ilovethisbook@ hotmail.com. Please, use call or text for emergencies! (This is in case someone loses a key.)

I'm confident that you're going to have a fantastic stay. I am also available for you via call or text at 888.888.8888 or via email at Andrew@Airbnbguru.com

Enjoy your stay!

Andrew

Here's what you need to know about your condo:

Upon Arrival

The condo complex is called Airbnb Breezy Terrace and it's located at 123 Sunny Street, Unit 456 (4th floor).

I will leave you a key under the mat outside the apartment, or arrange to have Cameron, my cohost, meet you.

You're going to receive two keys; one is for the apartment and another for the building common doors, which reads: do not duplicate. If the elevator is not working or under maintenance (not expected to happen) then you will need the common door key to access the stairwell and to get onto the floor (#4) from the stairwell.

There is an entry code that you will need to enter the building gate at 123 Sunny Street. It is "1234." This is just the numbers, no #. This code will open the gate and the inner double glass doors. *Save this code.*

Note—you will need to enter the inner double glass doors within ten seconds of entering the gate code, or the inner glass doors will relock, and you will have to go back and enter the code again.

You'll also find a small remote on the keychain. This is used for opening the garage, which is located on 4th Avenue, if needed, where we have included parking for free for the comfort of your stay. Additionally, this remote will open the gate and glass doors that I just mentioned by pressing the large button on the remote and aiming it at the keypads. This is just another way to enter the building in case the code does not work.

Laundry

There is a washer and a dryer in the condo unit that are both available to you always. Detergent and bleach are at the property and both are free of charge. If there is laundry in the dryer when you go to use it, please just set it aside for our team to take care of after your stay. (Whenever you are offering something that is more than expected we always like to let them know "for free" or "for your convenience" so they think we are doing a great job and can get better reviews. Remember, the goal is Superhost status.)

House Rules

By following these simple rules, you're going to have a better experience and enjoy your visit more.

- **Smoking inside the condo is expressly prohibited.** Please only smoke outside and only ash and dispose of cigarette butts in the designated spaces (ash tray or trash).

- **No unauthorized people at condo.** Please don't bring people to the condo unless we have discussed and approved them with you beforehand.

- **Be courteous of noise after 10 p.m.** We understand that you may be on vacation, but please be generally respectful of the neighbors, and please be quiet after 10 p.m. *No loud music!*

- **Please use the coasters on the tables.** All the furniture is new, and we'd like to keep it in great condition for future guests!

- **Lastly, remember you are my guest if you interact with the neighbors.** Refrain from mentioning that you are staying in a vacation rental through Airbnb. We want to make sure we're able to continue offering this fantastic space to fantastic guests like you, but not everyone is fond of this service. If asked, we appreciate your discretion and invite you to share that you're visiting your friend Andrew. After all, we are friends now!

Wi-Fi and TV
- Please see router for Wi-Fi name and password
- TV has cable and local channel service

Check Out Time
- **Checkout is anytime from 12 noon or earlier on day of departure.** It's important to adhere to this timeline unless we have previously discussed something different.
- **Checking out is super simple.** Please make sure everything is turned off in the condo, and lock the door behind you. We'll appreciate that you've cleaned your own dishes and not left behind a mess, but we'll take care of the rest!
- **We will try coordinating dropping off the keys to a host.** Please leave the key under the mat in front of the apartment if a host does not meet you. Don't worry—you'll know if they can ahead of time.

Contact Info
Andrew: 888.888.8888. Or email Andrew@Airbnbguru.com
Cameron (cohost/prop mgr): 999.999.9999 and his email is ilovethisbook@hotmail.com.

Please call or text me directly at any time if you have any questions or concerns, and I will be happy to help. This is what we're here for and your experience during your stay is important to us!

Thanks, Andrew

Thank you so much for being a wonderful guest. Please be safe traveling!

This letter clearly defines what is expected to make their stay a wonderful one. Sharing as much information as you can to ensure guests are having an informed, wonderful stay is good for you as a host, and great for your guests, too.

When I get this list of instructions as a guest, I will print them before I go so I can just go through them when I get there. As a host, you can always leave a printed copy of this sheet inside the unit, as well. There is no downside to this.

The Superhost

It's been suggested that heroes are ordinary people who make themselves extraordinary. In the world of Airbnb, an ordinary host can become a Superhost by showing that they go above and beyond what's expected—consistently—to give guests an amazing experience.

You can become a Superhost whether you are renting out a single room or an entire apartment or property.

There is an icon in the listing in a box that shows the mark of a Superhost.

You'll find this next to properties where the host has met the criteria to earn this. You can even search properties that are only held by Superhosts. Getting to this level is very hard, but well-rewarded when obtained. Earning this status means that you will have demonstrated a consistent twelve-month period where you meet all the criteria listed below.

1. **Commit to having an excellent response rate.**
   A 90 percent response rate to guests who are inquiring on your property is required. Airbnb allows a host to respond within twenty-four hours, but we always try to respond within an hour unless we are sleeping at the time.

2. **Host commitment must be shown.**
   This is important—you cannot cancel a guest's stay without reason. To earn a Superhost status, they must

have extenuating circumstances to cancel and not have it impact you. A few of these situations may include: deaths in the family, serious illness, a natural disaster, political unrest, damage to your property, and maintenance issues that make the property unacceptable for rental. It does say how many cancels you have. When I first listed my property on Airbnb I ended up canceling because I realized I was going to be in town, not out of town like I'd initially thought. The result of this was that it took me a long time to earn Superhost status.

3. **Have a history of five-star reviews.**
   Four out of five of your reviews must be five stars. This 80 percent rate helps demonstrate that you are a committed host, while leaving leeway for the occasional guest who doesn't leave a review, or the poor review that can skew your numbers.

4. **You need a history of amazing hosting.**
   To become a Superhost you need to have a history of ten completed trips, which should not be hard to achieve at all.

Ultimately, being a Superhost is an excellent way to promote your property, get more bookings, and as a result, earn more income. Very similar to becoming a Best-Seller on Amazon, once you become a Superhost, then Airbnb will promote you internally. Everyone knows how hard it is to get on the first page of Google and this comparison best demonstrates how tough it is to get on the first page of Airbnb.

If you are able to earn this status, aside from having the Superhost badge on your profile, you will also receive:

- ▶ Travel coupons for Airbnb after you've maintained the status for one year.
- ▶ Priority support from the technical staff at Airbnb—an excellent perk for when you're facing a technology challenge or have questions.
- ▶ A bit of clout in the way of having exclusive opportunities to preview new Airbnb services, products, and special features.

With Superhost status—which you'll absolutely want—you'll see which areas need improvement, as necessary, and how you are doing with your achievement toward it.

Enough of that. You will earn that Superhost status over time, especially if you really are committed to taking the steps I've outlined. You'd have to try intentionally to *not* earn it.

If you've earned Superhost status, you've likely learned the best tips and techniques to ensure you're masterful in hosting, all of which have been taught throughout this book. However, it's important to remember that this status is continuously earned, which means that you have to continue to be a Superhost to wear your cape—make that badge. Superman had a cape, don't you want one too?

Feedback & Complaints

"Feedback is the breakfast of champions."

KEN BLANCHARD

Just like a playwright lives and dies by the reviews given, so does the Airbnber. The importance of positioning yourself so you give your guests every reason to give you a positive review cannot be understated.

I have a friend who got to Superhost status within months by leaving guests chocolates and wine. Did this cost him a little bit of money? Yes, but the money he will receive from more listings and higher average room rental pay for that wine fivefold. This is similar to spending money advertising in a small business.

There are two types of reviews that are done for Airbnb hosts. One is the Overall Guest Satisfaction, which is rated on a five-star system. The second is the written review that summarizes their experience. Always strive for excellence in both.

The guest will only have fourteen days to leave you this feedback before the opportunity expires so don't be afraid to mention how important your reviews are to your business and let them know that you expect a five-star review, and if they feel they cannot give it, let them give you a chance. Find out why. This information is invaluable to you. Remember: it doesn't actually matter if you think you deserve a great review, even if you know that you've done enough.

Ultimately, even if a guest gives a bad review, as a host I should not look at this as a bad thing. I want to look at this as a way to learn and grow. This is free market research. Maybe it offers a way that you can improve on your place for a number of reasons, all of which will make it better in the future. I used to not have enough towels and blankets, so spending that extra one hundred dollars getting these things have lifted me to Superhost status.

Perception is reality for reviews.

The reason that you'd want to go through all this effort is that you are running a small business. Small businesses only stay solvent if you have a good reputation—especially businesses that rely on the internet, which is a home for people to be fearless and often reckless in their disclosure.

As someone who runs an internet-based business, I am always looking up my reviews and seeing if anyone is saying anything bad about me. They say that the damage someone can do on a review online is ten times that of a good review. Keep this in mind: you always want people to say positive things about you and your product. And as they say, a little honey can go a long way.

Feedback impacts your ability to achieve:

1. **Higher positioning in search results:** it's easier to feel confident renting from someone with great reviews and feedback. Therefore, it makes sense for Airbnb to put weight into this. Remember, if you can get to Superhost status, then the chances of getting a booking will increase because you will have front-page status. Also, would you be more inclined to rent a place from someone with one hundred five-star reviews or only six reviews, three of them bad?

2. **More clicks from possible guests:** great reviews combined with all the steps you'll take for a great profile and property overview are golden and invite browsers into your listing. This should be easy to understand. I am sure most of you have purchased something on Amazon.com, at minimum, this book. I sometimes buy whatever is top-rated on Amazon—regardless of price—because I know it will be good.

3. **Better conversion rates:** the data adds up and shows that people are more likely to book a room with a host who has proven they are reputable and reliable.

Components of the Overall Guest Satisfaction Rating

When a guest is asked to give this rating, they are going to be asked to evaluate six categories:

- ▶ **Accuracy**: we have already talked about this; it is better to be honest and accurate.
- ▶ **Communication**: a host is allowed twenty-four hours to respond, but I always try to respond within one hour.
- ▶ **Cleanliness**: this is huge. You are competing against hotels, so make sure you spend the extra money to get a really good maid.
- ▶ **Location**: you want to be close to bars and restaurants, but units in all locations are able to be listed for rent on Airbnb.
- ▶ **Check-in**: this should be a simple and easy process.
- ▶ **Value**: give the extra bonuses like coffee, tea, bottled water, and more.

Start by thinking about what you do have control of with this feedback. You can dictate:

1. **Accuracy:** make sure your property is what you have described it to be in size, amenities, promised little extras, and so on.

2. **Communication:** connecting with guests before, during, *and* after a stay is a smart move. At least offer it. Some will want more communication; others less. However, everyone will appreciate being asked about it. We are pretty much hands-off when guests check in, but many hosts will offer to take their guests to dinner, to coffee, or even cook for them.

3. **Cleanliness:** offer nothing less than what you would expect staying in a hotel yourself. If you do the cleaning, be meticulous and thorough, and if you hire it out, hold your service accountable. If a problem arises it's likely to happen when the guest first arrives. Make sure you have an action plan to remedy any concerns immediately. Offer a special extra for the inconvenience (gift card to the coffee shop down the street, and so on).

4. **Check-in:** this is your chance to make a face-to-face connection with your clients, or for your property manager to do it. Make sure you have a welcome packet prepared for them, especially if you didn't text or email it earlier. You also want to make sure the keys or keyless systems are in place, and that you look presentable. Greeting your guests looking like a slob is not reassuring to them. Once again, most of the time we are hands-off, because we all know how flights are always late, so we just do not have time to sit around and wait for our guests. To be blunt, shit happens.

What you cannot control is where your property is located and the guest's perception of the value of it, or their stay.

1. **Location:** hopefully you've considered location before purchasing the property if you're buying to become an Airbnb investor. You can get all this data from various sites, where you will be able to calculate the occupancy rate and the average room rate before diving in. Either way, if your location isn't 100 percent ideal you can still get good ratings in this category

by offering information for guests on transportation systems, schedules, and recommendations for great places to go that are easy to get to via that transportation. Remember to always talk about the positives, even if the location is not ideal.

For example: A five-minute walk to the train that takes a scenic fifteen-minute ride to downtown.

2. **Value:** this is the trickiest rating you're going to find. Of course, it's great to have five stars with it, but that can actually tell you something about your business model. If you consistently get five stars for value and have an 80 percent booking rate, I have to tell you— you are probably depriving yourself of some income. If this happens, don't be afraid to make a few adjustments and find the sweet spot. In the end, a lower "value rating" won't impact you if guests love what you are offering them. Cardinal rule: if you are not getting the reviews that you want, find ways to offer value. Your best resource to do this is from reading guest reviews. Many guests will make comments, and instead of being a host who gets mad, listen to their advice to make your listing the best possible.

Hosts can also leave reviews for guests involving three areas: cleanliness, communication, and observance of house rules. There's also an opportunity to give a "thumb up" or "thumb down" about recommending the guest. Unless something extreme happens, giving five stars is a smart idea. In addition to this, I also send a private message to my guests.

An example of a message that I might send is:

Dear Greta,

I wanted to thank you for choosing to stay at my property in Austin. You were a fantastic guest and I hope your visit was terrific. If you are ever in the area in the future, I'd love to host you again.

Have a great day.

Andrew

PS: I have already left my positive review for you to help you with future bookings.

This type of note is good etiquette that helps you to get good feedback, as well. It is simple and meaningful – and effective! Also, never ask someone to give you a good review. This might give the guest a reason to think about everything and not offer a good review. Most people, once receiving a good review, will offer one back.

The Written Review

Depending on what the guest was staying at your place for—work, vacation, or fun—they will likely add some emotions and personal connection into this review. By expressing how important their stay is to you and developing a sound rapport with them up-front you can create a better experience, which will lead to a better review. You want them to feel welcomed and show that their business matters.

My experiences have shown that this is the most important for the guest experience (in order):

1. Cleanliness
2. Accuracy
3. Quiet from streets (less road noise)

If all these are obtained you should get a great review.

Additionally, you have the opportunity to write reviews about your clients. These will help other Airbnb hosts, as well. To be frank, the single greatest way you can help ensure your guest writes a positive review for you is to leave one for them. To do otherwise would be foolish on your part. Even if they were a complete jerk.

You can't do much about a jerk (most of the time), but what are you going to do if you receive a complaint on your property? This is very similar to if someone gives you a bad review on the internet—show you care and that you value their business. How you respond is critical to the outcome of this.

"Customer complaints are the schoolbooks
from which we learn."
LOU GERSTNER

Complaints are never fun to receive, but there is a psychology behind dealing with them. For starters, you never want to argue against it, because this will get you nowhere in a virtual world, and even if you are absolutely right in knowing the complaint is bogus, it'll reflect poorly on you and your business.

In business, the expression "the customer is always right" should be your approach. What your heart may feel or believe to be true does not matter. So the first rule of thumb is to just accept fault and try to make it right. So many hosts do not want to think they are wrong and refuse to do this. By doing this you distinguish yourself from other hosts. Have you ever sold a house? If you have, especially the first time, you probably thought it was very special, simply because it was yours. To admit any fault makes you feel vulnerable. Just relax about it. In the end, being customer service-oriented allows you to diffuse a situation with as little negative impact as possible.

What would you do if you got this ugly review?

This *is not* the place to stay. There was a funny smell in the refrigerator and all I could hear were neighbors yelling at all hours of the night. And the bed—it was like a rock. It was a horrible experience and I would look elsewhere for your booking. You can find better for the same price, maybe less.

Dan

If you read this and your first instinct is to start typing away and throwing it back at the guest, the one you knew was going to be trouble, just stop. Most likely not all these complaints are accurate, maybe some are. Seriously, I can almost see the blood vessel popping out your head if you were the host. Breathe. Take a step back.

How you handle a complaint or bad review is extremely important.

Have you heard of angry texting and emailing? Also, the one that states you should never text people drunk? Damn, I wish I had followed that advice a time or two. You're so angered and distracted that you have typos, don't make complete sense, and are really throwing a virtual temper tantrum. These are things to avoid, which is why you need to dive into your logical mind when you're dealing with a complaint. "Just sleep on it." This means that if you are angry or upset, before just reacting on your emotions alone you take some time to allow it all to soak in. And to calm down.

You need to respond to these types of complaints and use these components in your response:

▸ Empathy for their situation. If you do not know what empathy is, you might want to Google it, lol.

▶ Gratitude for pointing out things you can address or improve. Remember, some of their complaints will probably be true, so this will help you become a better host in the long run.

▶ No casting of blame.

▶ Address every concern, specifically

▶ Some type of compensation that is reasonable, which shows that you are vested in *making things right*, or at least better. I like to extend an offer for a discount on a future stay instead of just giving money away right off the bat.

▶ A partial refund of their visit. Unless they request this, I would not do this. Some people just want to complain so they get a discount and this could be true for your disgruntled guest.

Factoring in these components shows that you have not only read their complaint, but that you are acknowledging it and understand it. I used to tell my ex all the time, "I'm sorry, you're right." Even if I didn't mean it. How's she going to respond? By calling me an asshole? I already added I was at fault.

It's not always easy having a business in the service industry, but as an Airbnb host, you do. What you say, and how you say it, matters.

The response could look like this:

Dear Dan,

I am as disheartened as you that your stay at my unit did not meet your expectations. I take these concerns seriously and would have addressed what I could promptly if I'd known.

Rest assured, I have taken action on what you've mentioned and done the following:

1. Had the cleaning service tend to the refrigerator to remove the smell.

2. Placed an order for a more comfortable mattress.

3. Addressed concerns with after-hours noise from the neighbors and purchased earplugs to offer immediate reprieve for these types of situations.

I am extending you a 50 percent discount to stay again in the future, should you choose to take it. I think you'll be delighted with how we've taken your feedback to heart.

Best Regards,

Andrew

What I am always mindful of is that mostly everybody in the Airbnb community is pretty great. I have been hosting for almost a year and I have not had anything to complain about. You will always hear those terrible horror stories and that is like saying that a bus tomorrow could hit you. Yes, it could happen but the law of probability is on your side. Guests are excited for a good experience and don't want to be an ass. This is great news, so when the occasional one seeps in, by no means does it indicate a rising trend.

Private Feedback

This feedback is wonderful, and ideal for guests who don't want to complain or mention certain things in a public forum. This will also help make your unit that much better, such as the guests who suggest more light blankets or towels. From this type of feedback, I've been able to add little amenities that make someone's stay nicer, became aware of a towel issue that I had (a lack of comfort and a lack of number), and am better able to respond to my guests with their concerns, which they appreciated as much as me.

Pay Day

The work is done. Once your place is furnished, we estimate about four hours a week per unit to manage it as long as you are not cleaning it yourself. This means by yourself you could possibly manage ten units.

I am making about twenty thousand dollars per unit a year before appreciation, so if I wanted to do it full-time this could be two hundred thousand dollars plus appreciation. Now this is some great money.

Your guest has come and gone, and their experience was successful. This is great, but let's be real, receiving the payday for all your work is great too. After all, you're running a business.

From Airbnb's side of things, they'll require about twenty-four hours to get your payment prepared for release. As for you, you have two options:

1. **Get paid as guests leave:** they leave, all is well, and you receive your money via your preferred method of payment.

2. **Get paid when minimum payout amount is set:** you can decide to have a minimum payout if you prefer. An example would be that once you have a thousand dollars in revenue in your account, it would be sent to you via your preferred means. I like to get paid right away, as no one makes the most of my money better than me. But that's just my preference.

If by chance you get one of those golden clients who are staying for more than twenty-eight days, you'll get paid monthly on those funds. Typically I leave all the money in my PayPal account and then on the twenty-eighth of each month I transfer money to my personal account. The reason for this is so I have money to pay the cable, internet, and mortgage on the first of the month. Also setting up auto-pay for the mortgage is a must so you don't have any late payments.

> Check your payout status by visiting your *Transaction History* page for your account. You'll see that this page also contains tabs for you to access your *Completed Transactions*, *Future Transactions*, and *Gross Earnings*.

Regarding where they send the funds you've earned, you want to evaluate which option you choose by determining:

1. **If they have fees associated with them:** depending on the bank you have or the means in which you get paid, there could be fees associated with your payment method. Verify, and if it's an unacceptable amount to you (for example, fifty dollars for a bank transfer or international wire) look to other choices.

2. **The quickness of processing time:** remember, financial transactions take place during the business day, which means you shouldn't expect a payment to come your way during a weekend or holiday. If you are in a crunch, remember this:

AIRBNB PAYOUTS	
Option	**Estimated Payout Time**
ACH/Direct Deposit	3 business days
Bank Transfer	3-7 business days
International Wire	3-7 business days
PayPal	1 business day
Western Union	1 business day (Pacific Standard Time)
Payoneer Prepaid Debit Card	1 business day

I wish Airbnb would take my favorite, Bitcoin, but hopefully soon they will. Remember the tax wisdom of keeping all your Airbnb funds going into one account, preferably an Airbnb specific one, to better track your business. Also, keep track of any expenses for the unit because you will write those off against profits.

You'll also get a chart to look at to see what you've earned over what you've estimated. You can go in and pull numbers any time you like.

Consider Attending the Airbnb Open

Continuing education and exposing yourself to the right people that get your business and can offer support and insight to help it is a standard business practice. The reason that I know so much about Airbnb is: I have taken courses on hosts and as a guest, read every book on the market about it, and used the product both as a host and guest. The reason I wrote this book is because there are not very many good books out there on *Airbnb: A 21st-Century Goldmine* and I hope you take advantage of this rare opportunity.

What's fairly new and exciting from Airbnb is that they have come up with a solution for their global host community that's called the Airbnb Open. I was supposed to go last year, but I had a speaking engagement in Las Vegas for trading. Despite missing it, I made sure to watch all the recordings.

This event takes place once a year and began in 2014. They choose a different location every year and the location is yet to be determined for 2018 for the event, which usually takes place in the late fall.

This weekend offers you the opportunity to expand your horizons and learn ways to conduct better business—and it's with like-minded people.

Imagine listening to the CEOs of Airbnb talk about the future and be able to rub shoulders with some of the best and brightest hosts all over the world. The great thing about Airbnb is that it is global and that every business owner can learn from others instead of thinking they are competing. Is my unit in San Diego competing against a condo in Sydney, Australia? No, but I am sure I can learn from that host if they are a Superhost and have multiple listings.

For me, the people I'm most interested in meeting now are the ones hosting experiences, as they are increasing and offer exciting value-added opportunities for guests. However, anyone can take advantage of learning and benefiting during this weekend by:

- Meeting other Airbnb hosts.
- Taking advantage of the insights of some pretty great keynote speakers and getting motivated. Every single time I go to a conference where someone speaks, I get motivated to make money.
- Learning how to make the most of your user experience on the Airbnb platform.
- Meeting the business owners who bring the services to your hosting that help you conduct better business.
- Having fun—hey, we all need some.

Even if you've been onboard with Airbnb since it first started, you can learn something from this big weekend. I particularly recommend going, if possible, if you are just starting out with your Airbnb investments, because you can't find a more energetic group of mentors that are willing to help you grow better. You never know, maybe you can find a possible business partner. Remember how I met mine, from staying at his place. Maybe you find someone in Australia, the second biggest country for Airbnb, and enter a partnership to invest in his or her next Airbnb.

This entire community really does prosper best when all hosts are striving to operate at an elite level. If you want to be the best at anything in life, you have to learn from the best. I want you to know a ridiculously large amount of information and use it to make money. I am an expert in investing, hosting, and as a guest in Airbnb so please feel free to email me with any questions: Andrew@alphashark.com.

Hosting Checklist

"I'm not saying the whole world will work this way, but with Airbnb, people are sleeping in other people's homes and other people's beds. So there's a level of trust necessary to participate that's different from an eBay or Facebook."

BRIAN CHESKY

So many people say, "I do not want to rent out my house or bed when I am gone, that's gross." Well think about it...The Ritz and Four Seasons. How many people sleep in those beds, and they do not sanitize them in between stays.

Take advantage of the checklist on the following pages to help you make sure you're addressing everything that is important to creating your listing all the way through the arrival and departure of guests.

Task	Overview
Assess Your Property	Make sure you understand what restrictions you may have with a property you wish to list, and decide whether to accept potential consequences, should they arise.
Determine Rate	By using the equations given, or the automatic pricing tools provided via third parties, come up with the rate strategies you believe will fit your business model best.
Establish Your Account	Create an Airbnb account with a solid, complete user profile and a nice, warm picture.
Create Your Listing	There are many steps involved in creating a listing, which include addressing: type of property, property overview, professional pictures of property to increase rental chances, thirty-second video for your profile, title for listing, complete description, amenities, house rules, minimum/maximum night stay policies, rush requests, advanced bookings, and cancellations. You should have a strategy in place for all these, and if this is your first time to host on Airbnb, I suggest you follow the guidelines that help people in your position.
Bookings	Determine if you want instant or manual bookings. Unless you are opposed to it, manual bookings can lead to a stronger experience with your guests, in which everything goes as planned. Why? It gives you the opportunity to engage with guests and ask questions, just as they can ask questions of you. However, instant bookings can increase revenues.
Welcome Packet	This packet is a great way to create a connection with guests, while reminding them of specific rules. Doing this face-to-face is good; however, you can do many of these things via email or text if you prefer. I also suggest leaving a welcome packet at the unit on your counter or TV stand. Remember to consider creating an Airbnb guidebook on their website that's specific to your property via location and activities in your community.

Task	Overview
Work Toward Superhost Status	If you're committed to using the Airbnb model as an investor, you'll want to implement all the good business practices that open this opportunity for you.
Manage Complaints and Feedback	Complaints need to always be managed professionally and with a "guest is right" mentality. As for feedback, don't hesitate to let guests know that you require it to be the best host possible, and that you'd like to know what you can do—if you haven't already done it—to receive five-star ratings and a good written review.
Insurance	Check out what is covered under Airbnb Host Insurance, as well as your individual insurance requirements. The Airbnb one million dollar-guarantee is not protection against theft or damage of clothes, jewelry, cash, and valuables. Also, you won't just get a check written quickly from Airbnb. It takes time and effort.
Getting Paid	It's important to set up accounts that streamline your payment process. Evaluate fees and length of time processing takes to make your best decisions. When you want to take out the money is up to you, but I try to take it out right before the mortgage hits. I also calculate my P&L on a separate excel spreadsheet and do this about once a month to see how my ROI is doing.
Tax Liability	You'll want to talk with your CPA or tax advisor if you don't currently have any investment properties and determine which way of managing the liability is most advantageous for you. I do not want to steer you in any direction because I am not a CPA.

Property Description Tips
By Jessica Vozel

It's well-known that to succeed at Airbnb, you have to pay for professional photos of your property (or be really good at photography yourself). What's discussed less often is what accompanies those photos: the *words*. That is, your property description, headline, and photo captions.

While even the most seasoned copywriters admit that photos capture a reader's attention first, you need more than expert shots to stand out when nearly everyone arranges professional shots these days. Plus, there are some aspects of your property that photos just can't show.

A great Airbnb property description accomplishes three things:

1. It outlines the factual information guests are seeking such as the number of bedrooms and bed sizes, a clear description of which spaces are shared and which are private, the exact distance to local attractions, and a description of the neighborhood.

2. It clearly considers what your target guests value and appreciate, and then succinctly communicates *how your property meets their criteria.*

3. It sells an *experience.*

If you have all three of these going for you in your property description, it's much more likely that guests will actually *read*—and not just skim—your description (or worse than skimming, click on the next one).

Have you got writer's block? That happens to the best of writers. Here are some steps to follow if you're stuck.

Brainstorm your USPs. Before you write a word, list going your property's *unique selling points* (USPs in copywriting lingo). What do *you* have that neighboring rentals *don't*? You'll build your entire listing around these. Include the USPs in your headline (and thumbnail image too) in the first part of your description, in the photo captions—everywhere! You want to be sure that your ideal guests find you and immediately recognize what you have to offer.

To determine your USPs, see what themes pop up in your reviews (walkable location, original art in the living area, ultra-comfy beds, and so forth). I also highly encourage that you research the listings of other Airbnbs in your area to be sure that your unique selling points are *actually* unique. An inground pool isn't so special if every rental in your neighborhood has one.

Focus on the headline. The headline and feature image (the thumbnail that appears in Airbnb's search results) create the all-important "handshake"—your potential guests' first introduction of your property. And it's competitive out there. Don't overlook your headline! In fact, consider writing your headline first, then using that to shape your entire listing.

The headline gives *context* to the feature image, adding important additional information that one photo can't capture. For example, the headline can indicate whether the rental is a condo or a cottage or whether that water view is of the ocean or the bay.

Remember: the headline plus the thumbnail image work best when they work together! So if you've got a stellar view of the Mediterranean, use the headline to feature it: "Endless Seaview Terrace Apartment."

Avoid hyperbole and cliché. Some words just flat-out fail to get your point across. Words such as *great*, *best*, *most*, or *awesome* don't sell a rental. You have to prove it with specifics.

Let's go back to those views of the Mediterranean Sea again. Which is more likely to sway someone: "Amazing, awesome views" or "End-to-end Mediterranean views from our landscaped terrace"? Paint a clear picture in a potential guest's mind by going beyond the well-worn phrases.

Think like your guests. As you write, make sure your potential guests are at the top of your mind. They're the whole point of this enterprise, after all! What do they want, value, and expect? What will make them Instant Book, then rave about your property with a 5-star review and referrals to friends?

To help solidify who your guest is, consider creating guest personas. This is a written document that identifies three key types of guests who frequently show up at your doorstep. Maybe it's the rushed mom seeking relaxation, the young professional who wants easy access to nightlife, or two friends on a foodie getaway, for example. Then write a few sentences about what these guests look for when they travel. You can even give them names and a stock photo face to help you really picture your target. It might sound a bit strange, but it works—trust me!

Don't forget: Vacations are an emotional experience. It's not like choosing a new kitchen appliance or garage door opener, where the specs alone will sell it. People save their time and money for months, sometimes *years*, for vacations. A great listing understands this emotional component and paints a picturing of what it's like to gather the family together for s'mores under the stars or dip into the private pool on a hot day.

With these tips in mind, your Airbnb listing can reach the next level, connect with travelers, and ultimately bring more great guests to your doorstep. Happy writing!

5

Be a Guest and Put Airbnb to the Test

"I think what's similar between a boutique hotel and Airbnb are three key things. Boutique hotels were really all about living like a local. How do you have an experience that feels like a local experience? That was really all around the food experience. Secondly, it was about having a design point of view so the design didn't feel generic. Thirdly, it was about turning strangers into friends. That's why we called staff 'host' at our hotels. All of these things apply to Airbnb too."

— JASON CLAMPET —

've basically talked Airbnb up as a huge investment opportunity, because it is. You've also read suggestions that recommend you actually use the Airbnb experience as a guest to determine if hosting is right for you, as well as to see how it works from a guest's perspective. It's time to get going and learn how to do this.

What does it mean to be a good guest? If you were to ask your relatives, it would mean to not overstay your welcome. It's probably not an exaggeration to say that Airbnb hosts may be much happier to have you—and if you are a great guest, have you back again.

Being a good guest means a few things. Honestly, none of them should come as a surprise, but hey, who am I to assume anything? Better to just say it. Trust is the heart and soul of what makes the entire Airbnb model successful. Or should I say, "Trust, but verify."

Setting Up Your Guest Airbnb Account

For a long while technology guys have gotten a bit of a tough rap, but let me tell you this...with Airbnb their love of tech makes everything pretty damn easy for you as a guest and a host. Even for those of you who break out into the sweats when you have to learn something new, you've got this.

We're going to go through each step, screen by screen. You'll meet my wonderful fictional friend "Take A. Vacation." This is one amazing person.

1. **The "home page" of the Airbnb website.**
   In the upper right-hand corner you will find a menu with five options:
   - No Time to Host
   - Become a Host
   - Help
   - Sign Up
   - Log In

   To be a guest, you'll go to the Sign Up tab.

2. **Pick method to sign up with.**
   You have three options for how you would like to create your account:
   - Sign up with Facebook
   - Sign up with Google
   - Sign up with email

   Which option you choose depends on your comfort level with that. Personally, I like to sign up for these things with email. We're going to choose the Sign Up with email option, so click on that.

3. **Fill in information page.**
   You will need to have the following information:
   - Email
   - First name
   - Last name
   - Password: I recommend you make it a password with a strong protection level. They have a password strength indicator right below where you put this in so you know.
   - Your birth date: you have to be over 18
   - Opt-in or opt-out: decide if you want promotions, surveys, and email updates. For this example, I am going to opt-in.

4. **Verify your profile details.**
   On this page, you'll verify that the sign-up information you entered was accurate and will be asked for a bit more specific information, including:
   - Gender
   - Phone number (and confirmation is done)
   - Preferred language
   - Preferred currency
   - Where you live
   - Describe yourself

Describing yourself is the most important part of this page, in my opinion. It's the first impression and the chance for you to get to really tell others a bit of information about you.

You certainly don't have to lie to make yourself the most interesting person in the world. You can create a description that shows your personality while helping you build your credibility.

Here is what Take A. Vacation wrote:

I have made a commitment to be good to myself this year. Part of this means not putting off the adventures that I know I want to have. I figure, why keep dreaming when I have the means to start doing?

When I travel I look for a quiet place to stay that's near the sites and attractions of the city I am in. I'm not afraid to be adventurous and explore, so I always appreciate suggestions for off-the-beaten-path destinations, as well as great restaurants. I have a big sweet tooth, so anything that involves a tasty pastry and a good cup of Joe is great by me.

The only thing that's high maintenance about me when I travel is my shoe suitcase. The first time the baggage restrictions were in place at the airport was, well, problematic. However, I've adjusted and find myself to be pretty content as long as I'm in a clean place in a safe location with a comfortable bed and good water pressure.

I'm looking forward to my first Airbnb rental and being a guest to this exciting way of traveling. I find it to feel rewarding to help a person make a little extra income and have that boutique hotel experience for a bit less money.

In addition, this page will also give you the opportunity to add in some extra information. The more the better. You never know what new options, plans, and incentives may work great for you.

Save your details. This wraps up your "Edit Profile" page.

5. **Add your photo and a video.**
   The guidelines for your photo are the same as if you were a host, and if you do both hosting and being a guest your profile will still be the same. So remember to smile and look at the camera, at minimum, and make it a high-resolution image.

Next is the video. While this is not absolutely necessary as a guest I find it to be a good touch. It allows people to get a glimpse into your personality and confirm that you are indeed a real person. It can also help them identify you when you book out your unit.

You'll notice that there are tips below where you put the video that encourage you to tell a bit more about yourself. Airbnb suggests to share:

▶ Where you are from
▶ Some of your interests and hobbies
▶ Any fun facts about yourself
▶ Your favorite things

The video can be tricky for some people who aren't used to being behind the camera or are hyper-focused on how they look. Just be natural and yourself and you'll be fine. Take a few trial runs at it, and if you don't like anyone recording you, do it alone.

Now you have a picture and hopefully a video, but there is still one more step to help keep Airbnb as secure a place as possible. This is step #6.

6. **Complete the "Trust and Verification" section.**
   You absolutely have to have this done to conduct business through the Airbnb platform. The sooner you get it taken care of, the better.

   Your email will already be confirmed just from the signing up process. However, Airbnb requires you to also provide them with a photo identification before you can book or list properties, as well as a second option, which may include: Facebook, Google, LinkedIn, or American Express.

After this, you will move on to what happens after you've actually booked and stayed at a property, which are reviews.

7. **Your history of reviews can be viewed.**
Reviews are important for the obvious reasons we stated, but they are also a reflection on you, which is important to remember. Make sure you leave thoughtful reviews and if at all possible are accurate in spelling. This just looks good. Yes, spell-check can be our worst enemy at times, but taking even an extra few seconds to double-check your review is good personal policy.

8. **If you can find credible references, add them.**
References are going to be most important if you do not have many of the other pages that help people find out more about you. These are your social media pages and LinkedIn, or perhaps your business page if you are a business owner. What you need to remember about references is that they should be:

   - By people who know you well
   - Speak to your character and reliability
   - Are done by someone meaningful (for example, your boss, not your doting mother)

As you can see, it's easy to set up a profile. I suggest that you write out your descriptions and longer details on a computer first using Rich Text Format and then cutting and pasting content into the applicable Airbnb box. This format is good to use because it doesn't make your question marks look like a box and some of the other characters not appear right when you cut and paste.

Searching Airbnb Listings as a Guest

The basics on how to search Airbnb for properties are pretty simple. A few basic search criteria, and *voilà*, the magic search engine makes amazing properties appear.

The prompts that Airbnb will ask you for include:

▶ Enter destination, travel dates, and number of guests. This should be straightforward enough, but take note that if you have a traveler that is older than twelve; they are considered an adult for search criteria.

▶ Click the shiny red "search" button after your criteria have been input.

▶ The insanely cool technology takes over and begins to pull up all properties that may meet your stated criteria.

▶ Scroll through the listings that appear. Another option is to use the map. It's your call and I think using both is a good idea. Not only is it interesting, but you can also learn a bit more about an area you are traveling to that may be unfamiliar.

Pretty simple and easy. You can also add filters into your search that will help you to hone in on the best choices of available units.

The filters can be a real time-saver if you have highly specific needs. Otherwise, it is somewhat interesting to browse through a few pages of listings to see the average prices for which properties, what previous guests have said, and if there is something important for you to know about, such as an event at that time.

On the upper left side of the screen you will notice that you have the filter options to:

- ▶ Select room type.
- ▶ Choose price range.
- ▶ Enable or disable Instant Booking properties. *Note:* you will see considerably less properties if you only have Instant Booking on.
- ▶ Refund policies (remember the six options, ranging from flexible to the strict).
- ▶ Additional filters for number of rooms and bedrooms, Superhosts only, amenities, facilities, house rules, neighborhoods, and even host language.

The right side of the computer screen will also show the map I referenced earlier. This shows the location of all the homes that are available for the criteria you've entered.

One feature about these maps that I find interesting from an investor's standpoint is how they show the average price ranges for different areas. It's good to know what you can likely expect before purchasing a property and this type of review is a good complement to the other websites and tools available to you for your research. Also, as a guest, it's not dumb to want a good deal if you can get one.

Below each of the property listings you'll see some basic information.

What's most important to note about this section is first, the Superhost symbol. If you would like, you a guest could choose to only stay at a property that has Superhost status, this is one of the big perks of being a Superhost.

In addition to this, you will also be able to see who is a new host and how many reviews all the hosts have and what their star ratings are. Check these all out pretty thoroughly at first, whether the property interests you or not, because it's good research. If you're looking at being a guest for the first time this is important. Additionally, if you are considering being an investor there is no more rapid-fire way to get what people are like with Airbnb properties. For the most they are awesome, but understanding people is not always that easy, unfortunately. It gets even tougher in the virtual world unless you know what to look for.

When viewing feedback think logically, first and foremost. Then look at the feedback and if it's negative, go a step further and look at how the host responded to it. This is where you will learn the most. Did they respond professionally? What solutions did they do to try to remedy whatever was wrong for the guest? A host who addresses these concerns is a host of character and a better bet than a host that ignores them. Remember, it doesn't matter who is right or wrong, it's who manages feedback best.

On the flip side, if you have a guest who is courteous and professional with concerns in feedback and the host goes on a rant, you likely want to avoid that host. It's not good policy and anyone who can't take a bit of nicely articulated critiquing has problems. Likely many more than Airbnb alone.

Let's fast-forward now. You found a property you are interested in and it's available for the times you'd like to travel. You're ready to take the next step.

Up to this point you have:

- ▶ Reviewed properties
- ▶ Found a listing
- ▶ Reviewed the listing
- ▶ Liked the price
- ▶ And...*you have some questions*

To get your questions answered you will want to click on the listing and scroll down to the "Contact Host" link at the bottom of the description. It's in a deep green color on the Airbnb website – as of today anyway.

By clicking on the "Contact Host" link you'll reach a page that lets you send a message with some details such as the purpose of your trip and with whom you're traveling.

From here your additional communication can start. If they do not allow for Instant Booking you can begin to inquire and build the relationship that hopefully earns you a booked room, as well as ask any questions that you may have.

If there is not a lot of detail on the property description about everything involving your experience the person is less likely to be a Superhost, but the areas that you may want to consider asking about include:

- If the property is kid-friendly
- Distance to the airport
- If it can accommodate any special concerns you may have (for example, Grandma and her walker)

Or, you can simply introduce yourself and be proactive and ask if the host has any questions for you. When you do this, explain why you're going to the area, who you'll be with, and some of the specifics about your trip. This will help the host better understand how they can be of service to you, as well as help you understand how you can be helpful to them in making a determination.

From there the conversation should go fairly rapidly, as you likely will not have to wait twenty-four hours for a response. If you do, and it bugs you, take a pass on that property because there is a chance that it will not meet your expectations. More hosts respond quickly rather than not quickly. After all, they want you to choose them.

Right before you decide to book the unit the one last thing you will want to do is make sure that you are good with their cancellation policy—and fully understand it.

The page on the website for all your bookings is excellent and easy to use. You can even print the entire thing.

What happens after you book your property is waiting, that ugly word that many people despise. As the time draws nearer you can expect to get reminders from Airbnb, as well as some possible updates from the host. I don't need to be proactive in a lot of communication with my future guests before they arrive. When it gets to within one week of their arrival, however, they'll receive their welcome packet and all the information. Between Cameron and myself—okay, mostly Cameron—we'll make sure that the unit is prepared and we are doing everything we have done to earn and keep our Superhost status.

Be the Guest Hosts Want to See

It would be awesome to just be a perfect guest naturally, and hopefully you are. To date, I've had many guests who were @#$%ing fantastic, and I don't take them for granted.

Although this is for travel and not relationship building with somebody for your job or personal interests, you should still take that same approach to being a good guest. For example, would you go to an interview and put your feet up on the CEO's desktop while you spoke? Probably not, and if you're at an Airbnb unit you probably shouldn't think you can just treat everything so casually like you own the place. You are, as your name implies, a guest.

Not to get too serious, but sometimes you have to be blunt.

From what I've experienced and seen from both sides of the Airbnb model, these are the basic things you can do to become a guest who will be well-received by all hosts as your travel adventures continue. The ideas begin from before you even book out a unit and carry on through to your departure.

1. **Read the listing thoroughly.**
   If you send a message to a host that asks if they are renting out an entire unit or a room, it's not going to reflect really great on you. This information is located on the bottom of the listing before you even go further into it. Pay attention. Additionally, read the entire description thoroughly. If you don't understand something, exactly, ask for clarification. This is fine, but to be impatient enough to go right to questions is a bad habit to have, not only in your Airbnb life but also in all of your life.

2. **Don't try to negotiate outside of Airbnb.**
   As a guest you've agreed not to attempt this when you signed up to Airbnb, and your host has agreed to the same thing. This platform is in place for a reason and it's important for building trust and ensuring that Airbnb experiences stay mostly amazing.

3. **Book quickly once questions are answered.**
   Of course, it's logical and suggested to get the "full picture" before you commit to a unit to book. However, once you get the information you need there is no necessity to keep asking the host questions or hemming and hawing about booking the unit out. You need to make a commitment and be decisive. This is especially important if the host has agreed to set aside dates for you or offer you a special deal. Action is what's required.

4. **Treat the unit with respect.**
   Hopefully you feel a sense of pride and like to take care of your own residence pretty well. Remember, you may be staying in someone's primary home so you should think and act in the same manner you'd want someone to act in your home. The Golden Rule applies to Airbnb, too: do unto others as you would have them do unto you.

5. **Inform the host if you are running late.**
   Although it would be damn awesome to, we cannot control the weather or the airlines. This means that at times we are delayed in arriving at our destinations. If this happens to you, do not hesitate to make your Airbnb host a priority. You should have their contact information on your laptop, in your phone, and so on. Be courteous and let them know, especially if they are personally meeting you at the property.

6. **If there's a problem, speak up.**
   You arrive and are set to do laundry, but the washing machine stops working. Let the owner know right away, not only for your sake but also so they have a chance to fix it. Additionally, if they live there they will need to know this eventually and you don't want it to look like you broke it. Weird things like that happen all the time. Again, this comes down to courtesy. You should want to and expect to know if something is wrong if you're a host, and be kind enough to tell them if you are a guest.

7. **Follow the house rules.**
   It's simple—follow the house rules. Period. You knew them ahead of time.

8. **Leave the unit the way you found it.**
   Your Airbnb host is not your maid or parent, having to pick up from you. Be tidy and respectful of the space, realizing that the condition you leave it in reflects on you.

9. **Provide feedback for the host.**
   I personally see no reason to ever have nasty feedback ever, especially if it is the kind that shocks a host and they are learning about your discontentment for the first time through it. If you go into an Airbnb unit as a guest to do research to eventually become a host, you have to approach this process as if it were a business research trip.

10. **"Heart" your host's property.**
    This is a nice extra touch that helps your host maintain and grow their good status. It's especially thoughtful if they are striving toward becoming a Superhost.

Most etiquette tips are geared toward the properties where you rent an entire unit. If you are renting a room in a residence or sharing a room you also want to be mindful of the courtesies that come with shared space, such as bathroom schedules, noise, common areas, cooking, and so on. This is basically everything you had to master when you had a roommate at some point in your life.

Make Money Anywhere

"There are also 'huge, huge' growth opportunities in the markets for family travel, luxury travel, and business travel. Business travel is already 11 percent of Airbnb's business, and Airbnb is 'just beginning to tap' that market."

— NATHAN BLECHARCZYK —

Can you envision it...a wise and elderly-looking person peering at you over the wire rims of their bifocals and adamantly saying, "If it seems too good to be true, it probably is." I am saying that just like the Gold Rush of the 1850s, it is not too good to be true. You just have to act fast.

It's been upwards of six years now that a fair share of people has either heard that or thought that adage about Airbnb. I mean, can it really be that easy to rent out a property you currently own or are considering investing in? And do it safely? The answer is yes and I have given you the blueprint. You're required to take the action.

The best ideas often defy the odds and old-time logic.

Airbnb operates in 192 of 196 countries and today people from across the world have begun to make a new choice. They now purchase properties that they stay at in cities and areas where they have reoccurring business to attend to. When they are not there, the property helps to pay for itself, making it a logical investment. The ROI an investor can get right now if they find the right property is insane if you compare it to a ten-year bond that is currently paying 2.5 percent.

Is it hard for some people to let go of the fact that their property is being used by someone they do not know? This is always a question I ask people, if they would be willing to rent out their house if it would help pay for 50 percent of the mortgage. For some, it is, and if it's a huge enough deal, then Airbnb isn't the right investment for you. However, if you realize that the number of horror stories and stays gone awry is extremely low, you're really tossing away a good opportunity on a "what if." Every person in this world is at risk of something crazy and unexpected happening when you least expect it—but this never stops you from everything you have to do or want to do. This is why I do not watch the news ever because it is always negative and it scares people, but people want bad stories so they feel better about their own lives.

Airbnb is as interested in good experiences for its hosts as it is the guests.

The idea of Airbnb was rooted in offering someone (the guest) a service they needed in exchange for some extra income that may help that person (the host). The founders of Airbnb only offered their place out because they needed money for rent and it ran from there. It has grown into a mammoth business, but at the heart of it, this is still the premise. It is currently valued at more than any hotel chain in the world. It's more practical than a sublet and it's more profitable than finding a traditional long-term renter for your property (most of the time). Also, before this, there has never existed an offering for a private room or a shared room. Imagine that being offered in the hotel business. Plus, you have this incredible platform that helps you out. Even if you don't know a lot about marketing, it gives you great, proven guidance and insight to cover those details for you. It's part of the deal. Setting up a listing on Airbnb is very easy to do.

Then you consider an environment with fewer regulations (at this time), a higher level of satisfaction for the traveler, and more space for the same amount of money – or less – than you would pay for a hotel. You cannot go wrong, and as the host, you get to determine what type of guests you want to attract and what you'd like their experience to be. Out of our three categories: the partygoer gets to cram more people into a unit that they wouldn't be able to in a hotel; the business traveler gets more square footage and faster internet; and the family gets multiple bedrooms, a kitchen and stove to cook, and possibly a cheaper rate.

It isn't often that you have a chance to pick and choose an investment to fit your needs, as well as the needs of the people who you rely on to make it profitable.

Airbnb helps people invest in real estate without having to be a big player in the real estate market. Most hosts are not huge property investors. They operate on a smaller level, using a specific strategy to deliver better results. They have an interest in the community or communities they own property in and this makes a big difference. About 80 percent of all hosts have only 1 unit and it can be even better if you create a plan to grow from one unit to ten units.

When it comes to communities worldwide, revitalization and promoting what's appealing about them means a lot. This is why the rise of the experiences and hosts interacting with guests is becoming an increasingly more available option, even if they are not onsite at the property with the guest. It all comes together.

What personally excites me is how we have a world that is becoming more socially responsible and the way we conduct business indicates this. Think of Toms, a company that gives away a pair of shoes for every pair of shoes they sell. Social awareness is growing faster by the day. Airbnb also promotes this by having adjustments in certain fee structures for properties and hosts that are interested in raising money and awareness for the causes that are most important to them.

I mentioned how education and giving children across the world access to quality schools and resources is important to me. Finding ways to help my Airbnb expertise make a difference with my cause is always something I am working on and mindful of. How can I take a portion of the money I profit and make the world a better place? How about you? Have you ever thought of changing the world, while living smartly within the one you have?

There's nothing wrong with making money, and when given the opportunity, doing something with the rewards of your investment does more than feel good, it feels great. It makes a difference.

So, in this world where we too often wonder if we missed our opportunity, Airbnb reminds us that we create our opportunities. And this 21st-century goldmine still has a lot of potential. If you don't take it, someone else will. And when you start to make money hand over fist, do not forget other people in this world who are not as fortunate.

The Revestor Platform

*"Visionary people face the same problems everyone else
faces; but rather than get paralyzed by their problems,
visionaries immediately commit themselves
to finding a solution."*

— BILL HYBELS —

All good ideas start with a beer...so I've heard and so I've witnessed.

Bill Lyons, the CEO of Griffin Funding, Lyons Realty, and Revestor, was sitting down with his friend Teevan McManus, and they got to talking about real estate. For all of you who know people passionate about real estate, this is probably not a surprise. However, the tone of the conversation and what they had to share is really what the story is here. For Bill, it was not rehashing the old days but thinking forward about what the industry could be. The past had shown significant shifts in how real estate was conducted. But what could the future hold for the industry? This is why a chapter of this book is dedicated to Revestor, because it shares the same vision that I do in real estate: the future.

The conversation continued. Bill indicated that he'd like to take his expertise and knowledge in real estate and detailed understanding of mortgages and leverage them with his passion for technology.

Technology was Teevan's passion and he had a belief that had stemmed from his work in the tech field. He saw technology in its purest form as something that should always improve a process. As we talked about earlier, having conversations about figuring out a celebrities' net worth without the internet. This is very similar to running Airbnb numbers without the occupancy rate and average room rental—it's impossible.

Up until this point, technology had been playing kind of a tug-of-war with traditional real estate.

Websites like Zillow and Redfin were in the game between real estate and technology, taking data and creating an impact. It helped people and caught on. In fact, today, 90 percent of people look online before they ever approach a realtor. However, these companies didn't improve on a process, they just gave information. Lyons thought there had to be more and he decided to pursue it.

I've shared information with you about how some people will be able see what a certain market will demand and others don't quite "get it" or choose not to. Revestor (Revestor.com) has created a platform that shows that they get it, even when other people do not quite grasp it. What impresses me is how they managed to combat the resistance in the beginning. We're not talking small fish resistance either. We're talking *Shark Tank* prime-time resistance.

Bill Lyons created Revestor with the idea of offering value to both real estate investors and home buyers. They could efficiently evaluate listings to identify which ones held the highest potential return. Anyone who has considered purchasing real estate has definitely been interested in this word: return. What's in it for me? If not now, later. This is the perfect solution to my need of crunching numbers. If I have a risk portfolio it makes it easier for me to invest Revestor provides this for me and I am going to walk you through the platform simple and easy.

The idea is sound by most people's standards. When I met Bill he was applying to join our EO forum. I said, "This dude was on *Shark Tank*. I @#$%in' love that show; he's in." What I did not realize at the time was that Bill knew more about real estate, investing, and mortgages than almost anyone I know. Bill applies to be on *Shark Tank* and he gets on. This guy is a great presenter, knowledgeable, and a good risk by all accounts. He is sharing his idea on prime time to some of the biggest players in the world when it comes to innovation and new ideas. He finishes talking and the feedback begins. Imagine his surprise when these guys could not even muster up visible excitement or rally support. Painful.

▶ Barbara Corcoran could not reconcile how it was possible to make estimations on value.

▶ Robert Herjavec looked at the concept and didn't believe Lyons even had a real business concept. He was out.

▶ Mark Cuban just didn't care for that type of business or business model. And referencing "didn't care for" is milder than what his actual sentiments appeared to be.

By all means, the idea appeared to be an epic failure, but there was one factor that no one could really estimate the value of, and this was Bill Lyons's determination and commitment to why Revestor was actually just what people needed.

No stranger to putting in what is necessary to make his dreams come true, Bill and a team of pros got to work on creating what he knew was an idea that people did need—even those who did not realize it quite yet. To fully get the picture, think back to the days before cell phones. None of us needed one twenty-five years ago, but today most of us are pretty sure we do.

Without the "seed capital" that a program like *Shark Tank* offers, Lyons knew that Revestor was going to have to go to Option #2—human capital. This meant giving "even more" in the way of a daily commitment of time, sweat, and blood. Not necessarily in that order each day.

Revestor began by marketing to a nationwide platform that was meant to go neck-in-neck with sites such as Zillow, a technology company that isn't a real estate company, and Redfin, a real estate company that isn't a technology company. There are others, of course. Revestor had already committed to being both a technology company and a real estate company. It has succeeded.

At first the logical marketing for Revestor was on a national level. They quickly realized that there was so much potential in what they had that it wasn't ready for that extensive of an outreach. It was time to reel it in and go local. This way they could improve and finesse on the platform to ensure it was relevant. A great example of relevance comes from Google. People search on Google for relevance. They don't put information in to not get something pertaining to what they want. This is what Revestor was focused on with its platform.

The data being received was not sufficient enough to optimally leverage the massive potential of what Revestor envisioned. Think of your personal diet. If you were to fuel your body with a crap diet you would end up with a sluggish and slow system. You would not be at your best. Trust me, I know this because I am actually a certified nutritionist from Cornell University. The same theory applies to data and how it's retrieved and analyzed.

Revestor rolled everything back and committed to a more organic data-driven approach that would improve the process. They decided to focus on investors for the site, as well. This created distinction and allowed them to really highlight how data could drive consumer knowledge and decision-making in the real estate industry. At first, they looked at just cash-on-cash return of long-term rentals, but as Bill studied the market, much like I do, he saw a huge need for short-term rental values such as Airbnb.

For Revestor, nothing shy of fast and responsive would suffice. It was going to be sleek, appealing, and draw attention.

The revamp began by focusing on San Diego, where Bill lived. After they were able to provide a value-driven service for that market, they would be ready to expand to other large markets by working with brokerages and MLS (Multiple Listing Service) who entered into agreements with them.

Are you seeing the San Diego connection? When I moved to San Diego that's when I met Bill. After hearing about his newest venture, I agreed with him wholeheartedly about the reasons why Revestor was needed. The platform offers innovation and excitement, giving users access to raw data and comparable that you cannot find anywhere else, at least not laid out in an investor-friendly format. Calculations and comparisons can be done for you based on your criteria. It's simple, and if you take advantage of it, you have a better chance of becoming a profitable investor.

The fact that they are a small start-up is one of their greatest strengths. They can pivot and adjust to what the market needs. This has proven to be a difference maker for them.

And in case you're wondering...no, I don't work for any chamber of commerce for the San Diego area. The service is worth talking about, and I'm someone who meets a lot of entre-preneurs with what I do. I'm excited to recommend Revestor because I believe it is a difference maker for the Airbnb model and how people approach investing in it.

Revestor will be launching its national platform in 2018. It's going to be exciting and offer endless benefits to those who want to try their hand at real estate investing, but want to have a better understanding of the process by having it more clearly defined. This is one more benefit of purchasing this book and understanding the need for this platform before it is even out. I am trying to build the excitement of every reader because I think it is going to be great and I want to make sure that you understand the platform as best as possible. Get ahead of the curve.

I am highly impressed with the fluidity and efficiency of the Revestor platform. It is revolutionizing the way real estate can be done. You'll be able to manage everything from a single source, from properties to financing to closing – and those ever-important calculations on which properties are great prospects for Airbnb investing. I personally like to always have comparisons in life, such as how much more money will an Airbnb short-term rental get me versus a long-term rental. I own a condo in Chicago that is a long-term rental and will yield me about 10 percent a year, about half of Airbnb, but for the most part it isn't any work at all.

A New Approach

Just because something has always been done one way does not mean that it cannot be done a different way in the future—an even better way. If you've ever searched how to learn more about real estate investing you have likely found a self-proclaimed guru at every corner.

"Pay me five thousand dollars and I will teach you all my secrets."

"Take this entire webinar series and you'll know everything you need to know."

The list goes on and on. Guess what you end up finding out? Oh, the guru business, love and hate it. Have you ever heard those commercials on the radio where they are looking for a few smart investors? If they were so smart, why wouldn't they scale up their business instead of teaching you the secrets for a couple of grand? Makes sense, huh? Everyone has the same secrets and tips and the only distinction, arguably, is in how they phrase it. Revestor understands this, which is great for you if you're trying to get real information to make big investment decisions. It's all about the data and revealing what the numbers tell you.

Success is found by connecting with a reliable source for data and understanding what to look for. What does the information tell you?

The old way of purchasing and closing on real estate included these steps.

- ▶ Search for homes
- ▶ Extract data
- ▶ Run investment calculations
- ▶ Have a thorough understanding of the numbers and what they mean
- ▶ Find a realtor
- ▶ Attain financing, which is impossible—lol

If you've gone through this process you understand how overwhelming it can be. Despite having top-notch pros and their good intentions working for you, things can go wrong. The odds go up the more people you have involved. This is what makes simplification—whenever you can obtain it from a reliable source—excellent.

Revestor offers one place where people can search real-time MLS data, adjust and run numbers, and calculate returns based off hypothetical scenarios for both long-term and short-term investment properties.

When I heard about this, a bulb went off, very similar to those cartoons I used to love. Instead of just guessing the occupancy rates and average room rental, I could finally get concrete numbers. This is when it's time for me to take over with what I do best, besides smile: crunching those numbers. You can save time, money, and learn a lot. Click a button and you can get a realtor who knows what you're looking for and the best resources to guide you along the way. They have looked at the long, drawn-out process and bundled it into one technology platform that allows for simplification.

Most markets have a certain type of investment property that's preferential for whatever reason(s). Having a way to connect you with the information you need more efficiently so you can run numbers on properties within minutes of it becoming a "live listing" is a big deal.

It's not only people like me who are really excited about using Airbnb for investing. Today, only four or so years after Revestor began its process, it is making a huge difference. Now *Shark Tank* rejection is last year's news and this year's news is much more enticing.

An article was written about Revestor for *Forbes'* online Entrepreneurs section. The title of the article from March 30, 2017, shows what a contender Revestor is now: "This Real Estate Startup Is Exploiting Zillow And Airbnb's Blind Spot."

This is a powerful headline, written by Julian Mitchell, whose tag line is, "I cover entrepreneurs and startups disrupting industries."

This article solidifies what I've grown to know about Revestor and the CEO—hell, the entire staff: commitment to this pro-consumer platform. It is literally the only real estate platform I personally know that caters to what the consumer needs, not to the realtors and lenders who are trying to capture leads first and foremost. Leads are important, yes. We all want them. But taking care of people like us who are interested in investing in real estate is important, too.

According to Lyons, "Big-name real estate franchises like Keller Williams, RE/MAX, Sotheby's, and Coldwell Banker are all deciding on how they will become tech companies. Will they hire large in-house teams of developers to build proprietary products, or will they outsource it to professionals who can keep them under budget? Bottom line, the space is getting disrupted. Just like Revestor, Airbnb is a disruptor in the hotel market, similar to Uber to the taxi market. If you think of either of these two companies, neither own anything, they own technology, a platform, and now a massive user base. If you adapt to change, the opportunities are endless. If you resist, you won't survive." I know this personally with Alpha-Shark because I have pivoted my company so many times. We have sold over ten thousand courses, but now traders do not want courses, they want indicators with buy and sell signals. This is going to happen and from the way I look at it from my Airbnb expertise point of view is that I will take the pioneer – the prospector who sees the future – over those who come in when the find is already over.

Long-Term versus Short-Term Rentals

Since real estate investing became a thing—basically since the time the first city existed on this earth—people typically looked at real estate investing with two specific goals in mind. I have properties that are short-term rentals and others that are long-term, depending on the seasonality of the location.

1. Find an ideal and reliable tenant
2. Hope they stay in your property a long time

It mostly remained this way until about 2008. Only then did perceptions start to shift, because everyone began to hear about Airbnb (although they are not the only short-term lease site). You couldn't help but wonder about it; at minimum, be interested.

Suddenly, short-term leases began to generate some excitement. They could be profitable instead of problematic. It made a difference. Revestor has given people who are curious about this the chance to compare what is different, exactly, between a short-term and long-term lease property. It's an incredible tool that you can use for a side-by-side comparison. Airbnb has done an amazing job taking away listings and properties from sites such as vrbo.com and homeaway.com with their Superhost status and easy three-step click to purchase system.

There's one other caveat to consider. The term "real estate market" is a huge generalization. Every city has pockets and neighborhoods, pluses and minuses. You need to understand where you're looking for real estate and what it can mean from an investment standpoint.

Depending on location, as well as neighborhoods, schools, side of the street, cul-de-sac, zip code, and so on, you may be blocks away from what is best suited for one type of rental over the other. Additionally, some markets are great for long-term rental but have excellent pockets for short-term rentals within them.

For example, the San Diego suburb known as Coronado has a very strong Navy presence. However, the city doesn't allow rentals that are less than twenty-eight days in length. Trust me, I know this, because I wanted to purchase a property there for Airbnb. Because of this, long-term vacation rentals work well there, as the military personnel get a monthly stipend of around 4,200 dollars on average. Smart investors know that they can rent out a nice place in this area for 3,995 dollars and likely get a great Navy family. With Revestor's platform you can run the numbers on that right on the site and see how it could play out for you. If money is ultimately the name of your game, don't just assume that long-term is better. You have to be smart and savvy about it.

The same thing goes if there is a short-term rental opportunity. You may have a huge influx from Arizona and Mexico City in the San Diego area. Even if you have an eight-day minimum stay, you could cover an entire month's worth of mortgage payments, maybe more, by offering a short-term rental on your own property. There are people who rent out their homes for an entire month from anywhere from fifteen thousand to twenty thousand dollars. Not too bad for a month's work.

Let's run a hypothetical.

▶ You are interested in a property in the San Diego beach area with a price point of five hundred thousand dollars.

- ▸ The fixed expenses you know about include 1.25 percent property taxes, one hundred dollars for insurance, and 250 dollars for HOA.

You do a little research on this property and learn the following things:

- ▸ On Airbnb, a property like this and in this location rents for 185 dollars per day during the time of year you are in.
- ▸ On average, you achieve a 60 percent occupancy rate for the property, factoring in prime times and slower times.

Then you evaluate between short-term and long-term rentals, discovering this information:

- ▸ With a long-term rental I can average two thousand dollars per month rent and have a full-time tenant. However, this will come at a loss of about one thousand dollars per month (no appreciation is factored in here).
- ▸ With a short-term rental in July, I can make about 3,995 dollars per month and average 1,700 dollars per month on the investment.

Revestor's platform allows you to toggle back and forth between short-term and long-term leases, while adjusting price points to see what works best for you.

I personally need to get at least double for an Airbnb property versus a long-term rental, because that long-term rental does not require much work at all. For me to invest, without appreciation, I want to get at least 8 percent ROI for long-term rentals and 16 percent for Airbnb. Now that I've used this system it's hard to believe that it's only first becoming available. We use a similar type system for other things in our life. Take buying a car, for example. If we buy or sell a used vehicle we don't hesitate to go to KBB, Cars.com, Edmunds, and so on to do our research. We check out our area, averages, and all other details that can help us be wiser with our decision.

Revestor helps you become the prospector who is panning for gold.

When you're panning for gold you're going to go to the hot areas and create your claim (that is, purchase that sound investment property). You can pinpoint and define your criteria and set up parameters and notifications that allow all property that meet your criteria to be sent to you as it comes out. Right away. No waiting until you have some free time or relying on a person to send you information immediately. When the market is hot, anything less than immediate is often going to lose out. Reality, folks.

Also, an account with Revestor is free and the site is updated continuously, 24/7. This is great, because we all know everyone loves things that are free, including myself. When something hits the market, Revestor gets it immediately and passes it along if it fits your search criteria. The properties that are potentially the right fit for you based on what your input criteria are will come to you via an email. We're all busy and for me this means taking advantage of opportunities that help make my goals and purpose easier. I get so excited to get that email, because I know there is a potential property that I could be investing on within weeks. It's this simple.

Revestor is...

- ▶ Efficient
- ▶ Easy to use
- ▶ Constantly updating data
- ▶ A single source for all the information you need
- ▶ An effective comparison tool for properties and various types of rentals

In a time-conscious world, this appeals to investors and busy individuals alike. Additionally, Revestor is creating value for the consumer and already for the future consumer. As this world changes and technology can be used to save us time, instead of distracting our time, it's going to get even better. I always say that time is money. Think about it, what would you do if you had an extra fifteen minutes in the day, hour, or even three hours? Furthermore, the company is very consumer-responsive. A big plus. What I mean by this is that they want to hear feedback, engage the end-user, and make sure that they are looking at the platform from all angles. You don't have to be a techie to see that a certain something might add value. You don't need to be a banker to know how to run the calculations that impact your decision-makings. All you need to think about is accessing a simple platform that will allow you to input some basics and begin putting the process into motion.

"With technology and Revestor the paint is never dry. We listen to our customers (the consumers) to build the platform based on their feedback. This is why the paint is never dry. We're always working on it and always good to improve, whether it's usability or data points, or something else. It's constantly improving on customer's experiences and predicting trends and needs...not just responding to them once they are there."

TEEVAN MCMANUS, REVESTOR BUSINESS DEVELOPMENT

Using Revestor.com

If you're adamant about not setting up a free account you can still use some of the features that Revestor offers; however, you are losing the true value of what they created just for current investors and future investors. The "no account" option gives you these assumptions to work from when running numbers:

- ▶ 20 percent down payment
- ▶ Thirty-year loan term
- ▶ 4.75 percent interest rate
- ▶ Three-year ARM (adjustable rate mortgage)

This information is helpful, of course, but even being off 1 percent in interest rates can make a difference. This is why you should take advantage of more information. There are so many factors that will play a part for your interest rate, such as credit score, income, assets, liabilities, and more. You're not playing around when you are considering buying an investment property. You can be the one who is the be-all and end-all of fun, but you still have to take some things seriously.

This entire next section is going to walk you through how to set up your account and how the screens look as you walk through it. I am a very visual person and if I do not have a step-by-step of what to do, I will probably quit or throw my computer against the wall, and this is why we have provided this for you. Additionally, you'll learn about the dashboard and the features it offers. The one thing you can be assured of is that this is a user-friendly platform, and I'm yet to meet someone who can't easily navigate it.

1. **Revestor.com Home Page.**
   Look to the upper right-hand corner of the screen and you'll see this sections that let you advertise, sign in and sign up.

2. **Click on the Sign Up link.**

    A pop-up box will appear for you and there will be a large blue button that reads: Sign Up. You'll also have the option of clicking Facebook to enroll. This is a great feature; I love hitting the login through Facebook option on almost every new company I join so I do not have to set up another password that I will probably forget. Since not everyone uses Facebook we're going to demonstrate how to do this by using the Sign Up button.

    You will need to put the following information into the pop-up box:
    - Email address
    - Password

    Then press the Sign Up button.

3. **Take a look at your welcome letter.**

    Go to your sign-up email you used and you will find your welcome letter. Today, this is what it reads like.

Thanks for signing up with Revestor (Real Estate + Investor = Revestor). We think you'll like what we've done and what we have in the works.

What We've Done Already

We've made Revestor **FREE**. Now you can find real estate investments in San Diego by searching for a city or zip code directly from our homepage. Revestor uses its patent pending algorithm to display properties that have the highest potential returns. Don't like Revestor's default settings? Then simply click on 'Refine/Save Search' to enter your specific investment criteria and let Revestor go to work.

Revestor's New Platform

We have been working hard on developing new features that our real estate investors want.

A Mobile-Friendly user experience. Revestor is now available on all browsers and all devices!

Saved Searches. When new properties hit the market that match your saved search criteria, we alert you. We receive 10,000-20,000 new listings per day.

Revestor is now easy to use, even for first-time real estate investors. Review our methodology, definitions & glossary.

More Data. We now have access to Sandicor data and update listings every hour. This is a huge feature, because some real estate websites only update about once a week.

Do you have a feature you'd like to see us add? Then drop a suggestion to **info@revestor.com**.

Happy hunting,
The Revestor team

See, pretty hassle-free.

4. **Back to the website...click on the Profile page.**
   When you first get to this page you're going to see the layout of what you'll eventually be able to reference back to after running searches.

5. **Time to run a search, let the party begin.**
   In the upper left-hand corner of the website you'll see a search box for starting to evaluate properties. In gray letters, they show what you can enter for your initial search criteria.
   - Address
   - City
   - Zip code

We're going to start basic and put in Coronado, California. Have you ever been to the dog beach there? Or how about the brunch at Hotel del Coronado? Amazing, I highly recommend it. If we were to add zip codes we'd already have to know which were most favorable, as there are five.

6. **Your initial search will pop up.**
   This screen is quite exciting. A list of all the properties that meet that first general criteria will show up, along with a spreadsheet that has the following columns on it:
   - Cash flow and cap rate
   - Specific address or particular street name
   - City
   - Type of property
   - Price
   - Number of beds and baths
   - Square feet and price/square foot
   - Year built

You'll notice, as well, that the top of the page indicates that it is a long-term rental, and so you'll see brackets around the numbers, indicating a monthly loss. A loss? No, Andrew, I bought this book because I am trying to make money. Do not worry. I will show you the way.

You'll also find a map on the top of this page that shows where all the properties are located, using markers on it. They use Google Maps, which is considered the most reliable. You can click on any marker and it will pull up the property that is there. This is ideal for searches in specific areas.

So far, we've done a vague search. What we are going to do next is:

▶ Switch to short-term rentals to keep with our Airbnb focus in this book. Back to profitability, thanks Airbnb.
▶ Set our criteria.

7. **Refine/save search.**
You will find this link to the right of the general property search box. There's a small home next to it to help identify it.

Press this link and a box will pop up with a few features on it that allow you to refine your search and save any searches you like upon completion. One tab will be geared toward your "Property Filters" and the next toward your "Investment Filters."

You'll find all the information you need to begin determining which price points and options/features are going to work the best for you. For the sake of our search example and considering Airbnb we will be *eliminating* the following criteria:

• *Listing type:* Fixer-upper
• *Property type:* Two to four units and "Other." (*Note:* "other" often means "unique," which can lead to financing problems or a lack of comparables to determine a good value for real estate investing. With this being said, many people love unique properties, as I've mentioned.) Remember us discussing tree houses being hot right now for Airbnb?

Then the right part of the pop-up box addresses investment criteria, specifically. You'll have the opportunity to make adjustments and set your parameters for these areas:

- *Rental type:* Short-term or Long-term rental
- *Income:* a) How much rent you can collect either daily or monthly, depending on short-term or long-term rental. If this is not put in, Revestor will perform a calculation for you. b) What is the target monthly or yearly occupancy rate? Again, if you don't put this in, Revestor will perform a calculation for you. My recommendation: use one of the Airbnb services to get average rents so you are putting in realistic figures for your price range and expectations.
- *Financing:* a) What interest rate can you get? [You can do this easily with a preapproval number.] b) What's the length of your mortgage? c) What are you going to put down?
- *Minimum required return:* a) What's the minimum cap rate? b) What's the minimum monthly cash flow? c) What's the minimum cash-on-cash return?

I'm going to run an Airbnb, which includes setting these criteria:

- Short-term rental
- Price range of four hundred thousand dollars to five hundred thousand dollars
- Two bedrooms
- Minimum of 1.5 bathrooms
- One thousand square feet minimum
- Condo/townhouse
- Rent per day of 181 dollars minimum
- Sixty percent occupancy rate
- Thirty-year mortgage at 4 percent with 20 percent down
- Five percent minimum cap rate

- Minus one hundred dollars minimum monthly cash flow
- Twelve percent minimum cash-on-cash return

When these criteria are on (which are based on some of the specifics I shared throughout the book), you'll then run the search. The results for this show a much more refined search, which will show favorable returns.

From here, using the platform that Revestor has for you to access, combined with the data that you're receiving about Airbnb averages from whatever other sources you have, and you've found a program that is going to assist you by saving you time and wasted energy, while not veering from the set criteria you have for your investments. Remember, the key is to take the money that you work so hard to get and to invest it wisely to bring back more money.

8. **Save your searches.**

   Save your searches as you begin going through this process. Label and name them however you like. When you do, you'll be able to go back and access them at any time. I've done searches before that I did not save and it is annoying when I have to go back and restart them all.

   If you decide to compare what it would be like to do short-term rentals on a three-bedroom property compared to a two-bedroom you can adjust those parameters, see what comes up, and save that search for comparison.

9. **Go to your "Profile" on the website.**

   The profile is in the upper right corner of the main page of the website. Click this link and you'll see two choices: Saved Properties or Saved Searches. If you go to searches, you'll see a listing of them.

Now you have access to information that you have already collected. You can delve in further to any specific property, continue to search, or begin to eliminate what you know doesn't work for your investment platform. When your criteria are put in and you opt for emails, Revestor will send information to you on any properties that come to market immediately. They will be ones that meet your criteria. Want to change your criteria? Just change your search.

You've done the general search and now you'd like to find out some more specifics on a property that is particularly appealing to you. You see a property that is very interesting to you and that is located in the Gaslamp Quarter. Wow, you have been listening because San Diego is very hot right now for Airbnb. You click on the marker on the map and you'll see a pop-up box like this appear.

You'll see four options at the bottom of the pop-up that has the property's exterior image. The first two are the "Cap Rate" and the "Price." The next two are "Save" and "Details."

Press "Save" if you want this specific property in your Profile so you can access this, in addition to property searches.

If you press "Details" you'll go into an MLS page that gives you extensive details on the property, including:

▶ Photos
▶ Map
▶ Street view
▶ Summary
▶ Similar rentals

In addition, Revestor provides you with an extensive overview that includes extensive detailed information that puts all your data in one place. This screen is where you really can begin to make decisions and answer questions.

Short-Term Rental View

When you press "Details" and scroll down on the computer Revestor gives a distinctive edge to your search.

Note: You can adjust details on the website at this point, as well, and run fresh calculations. These details are all ones that can be adjusted so you can further tweak numbers and see what properties work for you. You also receive a detailed payment screen for the property.

PS: in case you're wondering why it's hard to read the top number, that's what a red number—a monthly loss—does. Hard to read and for an investor it's also hard to swallow. After you finish this book, I will help guide you to never seeing that ugly red number on the top.

By the time you are done with experimenting with Revestor, even if you don't live in the San Diego area, you are going to understand the numbers game of real estate investing a lot better. And you'll be grateful for it.

I've made several references about the importance of knowledge and that if you are going to invest in something you don't want to go about it in a haphazard manner. With tools like what Revestor has you gain even more control of how your finances play out. Better yet, you can go into finance meetings with solid information and a better understanding about how short-term rentals work compared to long-term rentals.

I run AlphaShark.com and I want to invest in Facebook Ad Campaigns. Can you imagine how amazing it would be if they were to predict my revenues in the future based on my spending? There is not one digital marketing agency in the world that would ever do that; they can tell me my CPL, cost per lead, CPC, cost per click, and other KPIs, key performance indicators but not my revenues. This is exactly what Revestor does for me and this is why I call it my hidden gem and one of the many secrets to success. Remember, if you ever have any questions please feel free to reach out to me at Andrew@ alphashark.com

Visit www.Revestor.com and explore the site. In addition to what I've shared, they have a lot of great areas that offer explanations to help you better understand their methodology.

Resources that Specialize In Airbnb

"At Airbnb we're trying to build a culture that supports details, celebrates them, and gives our teams' creative license to pursue them."

— JOE GEBBIA —

As the number of Airbnb hosts and guests continue to rise, the need for services to help streamline the demand becomes more necessary. This list is not inclusive of every provider out there, nor is any of the sites on here an endorsement by me for their services. You can find services that will coordinate and book your maid around your booking dates or get that keyless door entry you need to book your place while traveling the world.

Before you make any decisions on which services may best enhance your Airbnb service, you'll want to invest your best efforts and investigate them online first. From this effort you'll be able to tell:

1. Who has the best reputations, based on the feedback you can find through Yelp, Facebook, and other consumer rating agencies.

2. The pricing for their services in comparison to others. If they are less, why? If they are a lot more, what else do they offer?
3. Which companies have the services that best fit your needs? Not all companies offer the same services. Check it out.
4. How serious and professional they are. This is easy to tell from your first impression of their website.
5. If they can provide the level of service you want in the area your property is located. Not all services serve all areas.

There are websites that I use and there are others that I don't use. Again, this is to aid you in your research.

Company	Service	Website
AirDNA	Analytics	Airdna.co
Pricelabs	Analytics	Pricelabs.co
Beyond Pricing	Analytics	Beyondpricing.com
Everbooked	Analytics	Everbooked.com
Mashvisor	Analytics	Mashvisor.com
FlyCleaners	Cleaning	Flycleaners.com
Proprly	Cleaning	Getproprly.com
Guesty	Guest Communications	Guesty.com
Nest	Home Automation	Nest.com
FIBARO	Home Automation	Fibaro.com
Lockitron	Home Automation	Lockitron.com
Pillow	Management	Pillowhomes.com
Urban Bellhop	Management	Urbanbellhop.com
MyVRHost	Management	Myvrhost.com
Airspruce	Marketing	Airspruce.me

Bonus Information

*"Information is the seed for an idea, and only grows when
it's watered."*

— HEINZ V. BERGEN —

This content is to give you data, as it is of the date of writing
this book, that offer you further insights into Airbnb statistics and information, as well as insights into how you can
make the most of your Airbnb investment opportunity if you
take it.

I really do hope (and believe) that this book has helped
you figure out how to list your property, why to list it, and how
to make money on an Airbnb property, whether it is your own
or an investment property.

There are a lot of creatives out there that are continuously
finding ways to make Airbnb a more appealing option for
travelers. Getting noticed is a part of the game. It's important
to remember this. What this tells you is if you have a hell of
a good idea that isn't mentioned in here, and if you feel it's
sound, do a bit of research on it and if it still seems good, give
it a try.

The new hot things that are very profitable for properties
include tree houses, small houses, and houses made of ship-
ping containers. You might laugh a little, but I am serious.
Airbnb listings for these properties generate a lot of business.

When people go on vacation, they want something different and that is why Airbnb came up with Experiences as well.

Interesting Airbnb Statistics

Some numbers don't lie, and these statistics are an exceptional indicator of why today is still a great day for investors—both conservative and aggressive—to take advantage of what Airbnb has to offer in the way of opportunity.

- ▸ As of July 2016, Airbnb had over one million users (guests) and by February 2017, that number was up to 160 million. As the Airbnb founders have noted multiple times, there is too much demand and not enough supply.
- ▸ You can rent an Airbnb property in 65,000-plus cities worldwide.
- ▸ To date, more females tend to use Airbnb. As of the latest statistics in September 2015, that number was 54 percent.
- ▸ Paris is consistently ranked the top city for active Airbnb listings. This is important, so if you want to travel there you can negotiate on price to get a better rate.
- ▸ According to Airbnb Citizen:
  - In cities like Paris, San Francisco, and Seattle, the host-and-guest community either approached or exceeded 20 percent of the population in 2016.
  - Chicago, Los Angeles, and New York City's majority-immigrant neighborhoods have seen 65 percent growth in active Airbnb listings in the past year. Remember, New York City and Santa Monica are not legal in terms of short-term rentals, and Chicago will

be seasonal, so expect to make money hand-over-fist in the summer and have very weak revenues in the winter.

- Travel and tourism has reached a nearly 10 percent global GDP with 7.2 trillion dollars in revenue, making this a bigger sector than the oil industry.
- Millennials and Generation Z will account for 75 percent of consumers by 2025, and they are embracing home-sharing experiences more frequently. You might feel like it is weird to be staying at someone else's home, but it seems like the millennials do not seem to care.
- As of today, millennials account for roughly 60 percent of all Airbnb bookings. This number even surprised me.
- In the U.S. markets, 85 percent of millennials support allowing residents in their cities to rent out their extra living space on Airbnb.
- One of the fastest-growing Airbnb markets is in China, where more than nine out of ten millennials say that travel is an important part of their identity. It should be noted that China is usually ahead of the curve in terms of technology, so this is why they go to Airbnb.

▶ Airbnb spends approximately 23.5 million dollars in advertising in the U.S. alone. The United States is the biggest market by country and Australia is second.

▶ The average number of bedrooms for an Airbnb listing is 1.6.

▶ At this time, the fastest growing destination neighborhood for Airbnb is Chuo-ku in Osaka, Japan.

Top 10 Getaway Cities in the U.S.

This list is compiled by Thrillist Travel, based on the experiences that a traveler can have in these locations and the availability of Airbnb properties.

1. Nashville, Tennessee
2. New Orleans, Louisiana
3. San Francisco, California
4. Austin, Texas
5. Charleston, South Carolina
6. Miami, Florida
7. Las Vegas, Nevada
8. Savannah, Georgia
9. New York, New York
10. San Diego, California

Other "hot spot cities" include: Sioux Falls, South Dakota; Kansas City, Missouri; Providence, Rhode Island; Philadelphia, Pennsylvania; Pittsburgh, Pennsylvania; Cleveland, Ohio; Washington, D.C.; Madison, Wisconsin; Santa Rosa, California; Boulder, Colorado; St. Petersburg, Florida; Asheville, North Carolina; Chicago, Illinois; Portland, Oregon; and Seattle, Washington.

Top 10 Getaway Destinations (Worldwide)

Some of these may not be a destination that would have occurred to you, or even be a part of your wildest dreams. For me, tree house stays are not of interest, but they are one of the most popular on-the-rise trends that Airbnb guests are seeking. What you have to remember is that you are now in the service industry, and it's not about what you'd do...it's about what you can offer others that can make you a profit while giving them a memorable stay.

Back to that tree house...would I ever live in one? Probably not. But would I invest in one? If the numbers made sense—absolutely. As I tell my traders, when looking at a stock chart, it should not matter what the company does, the chart tells it all. This is the same way I look at investment properties; I could care less where it is or if it is a tree house or small house, I just want to make money.

What do you think about these destinations?

1. Want to consider off-the-grid living? They have off-the-grid homes available now through Airbnb, and the most popular one is in California.
2. How about a brand-new mini loft in Rome, Italy? New properties that offer conveniences in some of the world's most beautiful cities are always of interest. People always want to try something new. I have been to forty-nine countries and I want to travel to another fifteen in the next fifteen months. Why? Because culture enriches us and makes us so much wiser and smarter. I always say, "I want to pass away when I am done learning. Until then, knowledge is power."
3. Are you ready to go Swiss Family Robinson? As I said, tree houses are a possibility for an investment, but one of the most popular Airbnb listings is for a tree house located in exotic and beautiful Bali, Indonesia. I have been to Bali and it is one of the most beautiful places in the world.
4. Have you ever wondered what it would be like to live like a pirate—a high-class pirate, that is? Well, the Pirates of the Caribbean home may be just for you. Once again, it sounds crazy, right? But many of these places are booked out for months in advance, even up to six months. You thought it was hard to get into

that new hot restaurant in New York City, think again. Getting into the pirate ship house is even harder. Another destination located in California.

5. Not all amazing adventures are city adventures. If you want to go rustic, there's a dome cabin that's near mountains, hiking, and a beach. Another intriguing property that shows the diversity that California offers to Airbnb enthusiasts.

6. Do you love wine and fresh air? Then you may love the tree house in Tuscan, Italy. Valleys, vino, and lots of appeal to go along with it. This is a part of the new platform called Experiences that Airbnb has rolled out. They forecast that these Experiences could bring in more revenues than Airbnb hosting itself.

7. Rustic living in some of the most beautiful wooded areas in the world—that's what you get with a unique cabin that's located at Mayne Island, British Columbia, Canada.

8. A tree house filled with floor-to-ceiling windows and views of the Florence, Italy, landscape. That's an option that may be ideal for those who want to bring the feeling of the city to their exciting adventure.

9. Long to be surrounded by an ocean feel? The seashell house in Isla Mujeres, Mexico, can deliver. Without a doubt, it's a one of a kind experience. When I go to Mexico, which I do often, I want to be part of the culture. I am going there to get away, so I don't want this type of diversion from the culture. That's just me; definitely not everyone.

10. Interested in a hidden treasure in the city? You'll definitely want to check out the secluded tree house that is snuggled within the city limits of Atlanta – and all the rope bridges that connect the three units.

The Most Profitable U.S. Cities for CoC Returns

Airdna is a resource that you'll want to make sure to scout as you begin making your investment decisions. They have great bits of information and the site is very user-friendly—always a bonus.

As of December 2, 2016, in an article put together by Daniela Andreevska, these are the cities you'll want to consider investing in, based on cash-on-cash returns.

City	Cash-on-cash Return/ Cap Rate	Occupancy Rate	Average Monthly Rental Income	Median Property Price
Breckenridge, Colorado	22.8%/ 28.5%	37.2%	$2,485	$168,000
Catskill, New York	16.3%/ 22.1%	40.6%	$2,779	$170,000
OK City, Oklahoma	15.7%/ 21.8%	48.9%	$1,754	$163,500
Hyde Park, New York	14.1%/ 19.5%	28.1%	$3,399	$224,500
Panama City, Florida	13.0%/ 17.2%	54.6%	$2,644	$177,000
Narrowsburg, New York	12.8%/ 19.2%	31.6%	$2,208	$147,000
Castroville, California	12.8%/ 16.1%	38.6%	$6,710	$489,500
Charleston, S. Carolina	12.7%/ 16.2%	53.7%	$3,693	$299,900
Joshua Tree, California	12.5%/ 17.0%	47.5%	$2,545	$179,700
Lancaster, Pennsylvania	12.3%/ 18.0%	39.3%	$1,934	$137,500

Note: Even though the cash-on-cash return might be higher in these cities than San Diego, I love San Diego because I am there in case something happens, and I think the real estate appreciation will do much better.

What I find interesting about this list and research is that it shows us something we may not typically believe to be true. I have heard of Joshua Tree, because it is a U2 album, but did you actually know that it was a city (about 125 miles east of Los Angeles)? First, the largest cities for real estate investors are not always the most popular. And, two, there are some pretty great locations out there that are Airbnb-friendly and where real estate is quite affordable. It's all worth considering as you evaluate your options.

Note: Before you even start, remember that it will be hard to own an Airbnb property unless you live in the city or have a property manager, which could possibly cost you 20 percent. So, start small and then you will be able to build it up.

Most Profitable U.S. Cities for Private Room Rentals

The ability to make money renting out an extra room is also an option for you to remember. It doesn't have to be about investment alone. If you have a garage or an extra bedroom that you don't use, you can make money for the mortgage, extra vacation, or even for that rainy-day account. At times, it can be enough to offset rent, get out of town if an event's happening that you don't care about, but can profit from, and a great way to make your own vacations and experiences more affordable.

Or, you have a choice to be there and play host to whomever is staying. Some people do this just to meet interesting people. Imagine that you are a little bit older, live alone, and all your children now have children. It might be a nice way to enjoy someone's company and make money while doing it. This is a more popular option than you may think, assuming that it fits your personality. That style of room rental doesn't work for me, but I know many Airbnb people (including my business partner Cameron) who are perfectly okay with it.

I know you might think I'm crazy for suggesting it, but you can always put a listing up once and try it out. Do you like chocolate? I hope you answered yes. Well, how do you know that? Probably because you've had it before. So hey, don't knock it until you try it.

City	Average Monthly Rent for Two-Bedroom	Average Airbnb Private Room Rate	Average Occupancy Rate	% of Monthly Rent Paid
Houston	$1,293	$70	64%	106%
Philadelphia	$1,489	$72	64%	94%
Chicago	$1,727	$75	71%	93%
Dallas	$1,305	$66	60%	92%
San Diego	$2,017	$85	71%	91%
Miami	$1,879	$91	61%	91%
Oakland	$2,140	$74	83%	88%
Seattle	$2,109	$72	77%	79%
San Jose	$2,469	$84	75%	77%
Boston	$2,796	$87	77%	73%
Wash., D.C.	$2,586	$77	71%	64%
San Fran.	$4,642	$111	86%	63%
Los Angeles	$2,869	$80	72%	61%
New York	$3,732	$86	80%	56%

Most Profitable U.S. Cities for Two-Bedroom Private Rentals

Two bedrooms seem to be the magical number for many Airbnb guests. Generally, your place will rent for 1.5 times a one-bedroom; do not think just because you have a two-bedroom that you will get twice the price of a one-bedroom, because this is not true. If they have large groups of people, many are more than content to sleep on air mattresses (especially if they are younger). They are looking for a place to crash, or have smaller children who are okay with this.

The trick for you to remember is to help accommodate all this by having pullout couches and air mattresses. Suddenly, a one-bedroom now sleeps six and the two-bedroom sleeps eight. This makes your place a lot more desirable.

City	Two-Bedroom Rate	Average Monthly Rent	Annual Expected Revenue/ Annual Expenses	Expected Profits
San Diego	$226	$2,017	$58,750/ $27,269	$31,481
Miami	$240	$1,879	$53,821/ $25,125	$28,696
Chicago	$184	$1,727	$47,525/ $23,3349	$24,175
Boston	$214	$2,796	$59,955/ $37,024	$22,931
San Jose	$197	$2,469	$53,575/ $32,490	$21,085
Philadelphia	$172	$1,489	$40,279/ $20,653	$19,626
New York	$233	$3,732	$67,712/ $48,399	$19,313

City	Two Bedroom Rate	Average Monthly Rent	Annual Expected Revenue/ Annual Expenses	Expected Profits
San Francisco	$247	$4,642	$77,845/ $58,566	$19,279
Oakland	$156	$2,140	$47,464/ $28,574	$18,891
Houston	$156	$1,293	$36,661/ $1,181	$18,470
Seattle	$164	$2,109	$45,823/ $28,012	$17,811
Portland	$140	$1,528	$38,535/ $20,771	$17,764
Los Angeles	$208	$2,869	$54,762/ $37,022	$17,740
Washington, D.C.	$192	$2,586	$49,868/ $33,593	$36,275
Dallas	$156	$1,305	$34,191/ $18,441	$15,750

Most Popular One-Bedroom Cities Worldwide

If you're looking for a place to vacation you'll want to consider one of these Airbnb-friendly cities. At times, I have thought it was a pain to get an Airbnb for one or two nights, as opposed to a hotel, but if I am staying anywhere for more than three nights I will 100 percent get an Airbnb because it is bigger, cheaper, and I can even cook my own meals to save money.

Or if your next business destination takes you there, this may be a preferred new way to travel and make the most of your experience. Perhaps investing in real estate internationally appeals to you, in which case these destinations definitely should be further explored. While I wrote that for you, I also caution you to really evaluate if this is a wise investment. There are many international cities that you do not actually own land, you lease it from the government for ninety-nine years. There are also cities such as Buenos Aires where you think that you are buying a unit, but it is really a scam, so I would be very careful.

This list is based off information published at *Forbes* online in November 2016.

City	One Bedroom Rate	Average Monthly Rent	Average Occupancy / Highest 10% ROI
Barcelona	$112	$787	71%/278%
Prague	$67	$592	68%/235%
Montreal	$86	$719	66%/206%
Osaka	$73	$732	70%/205%
Los Angeles	$144	$1,482	76%/203%
Berlin	$84	$762	70%/198%
Cape Town	$72	$637	64%/189%
Lisbon	$69	$645	70%/182%
Paris	$117	$1,185	66%/172%
Rio de Janeiro	$83	$673	58%/169%
Madrid	$81	$831	71%/168%
Rome	$101	$1,055	67%/161%
Toronto	$104	$1,164	74%/151%
Melbourne	$109	$1,240	75%/143%
São Paulo	$55	$601	67%/134%
Milan	$94	$1,021	65%/130%

Istanbul	$49	$513	55%/130%
London	$163	$2,083	71%/126%
Copenhagen	$123	$1,322	62%/120%
Seoul	$67	$969	74%/112%
Tokyo	$87	$1,243	73%/111%
Tel Aviv	$97	$1,129	65%/109%
New York	$176	$2,915	72%/78%
Sydney	$124	$1,940	73%/77%
Shanghai	$72	$1,483	68%/30%

Exciting Airbnb Experience Options

Vacationing and learning something new or of interest to you has become an emerging trend and it's one that Airbnb has really taken advantage of. Experience destinations continue to grow every day. I'm even considering creating an Experience Option for people who want to learn trading.

These experiences are not offered in every city yet, but I believe it will be huge enough for Airbnb that many options will arise out of the demand for them. I mean, if I go to Hawaii, why wouldn't I want to surf and eat food from a local? It takes you off the beaten path and into a real-time experience of the culture that exists in the places you travel.

As of this date, here are some of the most exciting and unique Experiences. You can see the ever-adding list of experiences by going to Airbnb's website and visiting the Experiences tab. A few of the ones that have received great reviews include:

- ▶ Cooking classes and pastry making
- ▶ Learning the art of urban gardening

- ▶ Watching marine mammals
- ▶ Learning opportunities for business and personal growth in smaller groups
- ▶ Music and the arts
- ▶ Fitness and yoga
- ▶ A day in Little Havana with a local
- ▶ Fashion and shopping
- ▶ Water adventures
- ▶ Off-road adventures
- ▶ Surfing lessons
- ▶ Historic sightseeing
- ▶ Bike tours
- ▶ Craft beer brewing
- ▶ Wine country tours and tastings
- ▶ Hang gliding
- ▶ Overnight hike with wolves
- ▶ Write a TV episode with a writer
- ▶ And more

Ways to Improve Your Airbnb Ranking

There are specific things you can do to get your listing to appear higher up on Airbnb. The search within Airbnb works like Google or Amazon, meaning that certain analytics are used, and those who are more mindful of them will appear higher in the results because of it. These are smart strategies to help you maximize the numbers you're hoping to achieve as an investor. It bears repeating—listings on the first page can get up to 80 percent of the bookings so it makes sense to try everything possible to get on the front page.

1. **Get verified.**
   People may be more willing to explore the world today than ever before and love the idea of house

sharing to create a better experience. Don't mistake this with a lack of attention to having a safe experience. Getting verified is an important step to take if you are really serious about building your ranking and showing that you are as interested as your guests are in their peace of mind. Think about it, would you trust someone with more or less information? Almost like a résumé, someone who has a LinkedIn profile seems more legitimate than someone who doesn't.

2. **Promptly respond to feedback.**
This is simple courtesy, but as an Airbnb host it is extremely important. People are trusting in you to provide for them and be responsive in the same manner a hotel would be accommodating to its guests. Poor response times don't bode well for you. Ideally, you should be at 100 percent, whether you respond or have hired someone to do this for you. You can check out your rate under the Stats tab under your Airbnb account page.

    Note: Hosts who respond to questions, queries, and concerns within an hour have a great chance at moving up higher on the listings. Customer service is king, which is why this is one of the most important ways to get a higher ranking.

3. **Use high quality images to highlight your property.**
Airbnb now offers free picture-taking in major cities so you may have the luxury of having them take pictures for you. I use this for all my places, but it is not offered in all major cities. If you are on your own make sure you are using a photographer who has a good eye and that you stage the pictures so they highlight the best features of your property. Your

pictures should invite people in, but not look lived in (your dinner plate in the corner and the toilet lid up). Always good to throw that coffee cup or Apple computer in so they can imagine themselves staying at your place.

4. **Create a compelling, detailed property profile.**
Have a thorough, accurate, and error-free description of your property. When this is combined with good images you will get better results.

5. **Encourage reviews from your guests.**
The highest review you can get is a five-star review. You'll want to make sure that you share with your guests how important this review is and that you care if you receive it. A warm and inviting message can also help you earn these valuable reviews. The more five-star reviews, the higher up in the rankings you'll go on Airbnb. Just be aware that you never want to bother a guest for a review, because that might bite you in the butt. However, trying things that are "review-friendly" like a bottle of wine from a local winery or a souvenir are good touches that will speak volumes for you. Anything that makes the guest feel that you are going out of your way will help.

6. **Promote being added to a "wish list."**
This is the one thing that is the most out of your control. However, being added to a wish list will increase your rankings. Don't be too shy to suggest to your guests that they put you on their wish list. If you've treated them right, the mentality of the Airbnb traveler will likely want to return the favor. It is a unique global community.

7. **Talk about the area you live in.**
   Sharing what's unique or special about your city or nearby surroundings is a wonderful way to draw in the people who are viewing your listing. Additionally, it shows guests that you are vested in the quality of their experience if they stay with you.

8. **Pay attention to your pricing.**
   If your pricing is out of skew—either too high or too low—compared to other properties in your city, you'll risk alienating potential clients. Too low of prices make people wonder what may be wrong with it. Too high of prices may exclude people from considering your property. Why pay more for you when they can get a similar property in a similar location for less? Once again, this is an acquired skill that you will learn over time, but one of the easiest ways to get pricing is to look at the competition of similar places in your area and how much they are going for.

9. **Update your calendar regularly.**
   Even if you don't have new activity on your calendar each day, it's good to visit it and make sure all is in order. This simple few minutes task can help boost your ratings. Often, we will change the price of a unit by one dollar, just if there is activity in the account, and sometimes this is just enough to move the rankings higher.

Eight Ways to Show Your Hosting Mastery

Regardless of the reason why someone is traveling and chooses you, it's the little extras that mean a lot. At minimum, they help you be distinct and leave a positive impression.

Consider these eight key and important tips:

1. If your target market is family, have a closetful of fun, family-friendly games available. You can also include some needed extras like a crib and a high chair, as well as a list of area pediatricians and drug stores. Monopoly, Connect Four, Chess, Checkers, and Guess Who are some of my favorites that are very popular with families.

2. Have some complimentary beverages available. At my Austin property, I keep Russian vodka and Patrón in the freezer, along with a welcome note encouraging my guests to enjoy some complimentary cocktails if they wish.

3. Get free passes to local attractions and businesses (such as fitness clubs or even a night club) to welcome your guests to your city. You can get these very easily and they go a long way with the guests.

4. Make sure your apartment is equipped with the amenities that most people would find in a hotel. In specific, irons, hairdryers, and a clean, fully equipped kitchen should be there.

5. If you don't mind spending time with your guests—which is a personal preference—extend an offer to take them on a tour or meet for a drink or cup of coffee. This is really effective for building a good reputation, but needs to be evaluated guest-by-guest. This is one I almost never do, but some hosts enjoy the company and love meeting people from around the world.

6. Have extra blankets, pillows, and towels in your apart-ment/home. Anything that adds to the comfort and convenience of your guests is a good thing. At first, I did not have these and I lost some rankings because of this, but these go a long way.

7. Consider offering free coffee and tea, perhaps even some breakfast essentials to your clients. An effec-tive idea that clients have been known to appreciate is a welcome platter of fruit and cheese, along with a bottle of wine from a local vineyard. Always be mindful of creating an experience that stands apart. I know I drink coffee every morning, so if there is coffee at an Airbnb I am staying at it just saved my five dollars and a trip to Starbucks.

8. A nice-smelling house is inviting and relaxing. Make sure you do light scents and not heavy ones such as cinnamon, as they can overwhelm some people. In real estate, a trick to make a house feel like a home during an open house is to bake a loaf of bread before the showing. The smell has a positive psychological response for most people.

Interviews

The following are five interviews from people involved with Airbnb and the three different business models on how *any* individual could make money on the Airbnb ecosystem.

1. An individual who is an expert in arbitrage long-term versus short-term rentals

2. Individuals who rent out a spare bedroom in their own home to help pay their mortagage

3. An individual who has rented a huge house they own to pay for a vacation

Expert in Arbitrage Long-Term versus Short-Term Rentals: Q & A with Cameron Eckstein

About Cameron Eckstein

When hosting, I live by the motto *mi casa es su casa* (my house is your house).

I live and work in San Diego, California, America's *finest* city, and I love the beach/surfing, exercising, yoga, golf, snow-boarding, watching and attending sporting events, and eating at new restaurants. I also enjoy beer/wine (San Diego has a great microbrewery scene)!

I consider myself outgoing, easy to get along with, *very communicative* and *flexible*. I've been known to make friends and spend time with my guests, if that's what they prefer, but also can keep myself busy and leave them alone (if that's what they want!).

Q: *How long have you been a host on Airbnb?*

A: A little over four years.

Q: *Are you a Superhost?*

A: Yes, I recently obtained Superhost status this year.

Q: *How many properties do you host currently?*

A: I currently host seven properties across three states. At any given time, I host anywhere between seven to ten properties across three to five states, and I hope to expand to fifteen properties by next year across six to seven states.

Q: *How many properties do you currently have on an arbitrage of long term versus short term?*

A: All but one of my properties is a STR and is taking advantage of the arbitrage between long and short term. The one property on long term is because there is no arbitrage opportunity available. This is for a variety of reasons, but mainly because the market doesn't support it.

Q: *How do you find the places that you want to exploit this arbitrage?*

A: There are three main factors to consider: location, cash-on-cash return analysis, and regulation. Regulation is the easiest to research, since it's fairly black and white. There are two types of regulation—government and community (that is, HOA). I prefer to be in locations where there is minimal regulation. Cash-on-cash return analysis is straightforward once you have a mature model; however, there will always be assumptions. These assumptions can be difficult to pinpoint, but there are ways to do so based on market research reports from services such as AirDNA, Airbnb itself, and local experience. I always aim to be conservative in my assumptions, especially when investors are involved. Location is the third, and probably the most important. It is tough because even within cities there are micro-geographies and it can be hard to gauge demand. I look for places that are walkable and appeal to tourists and businesses alike. Again, reports on this can be found through third-party services like AirDNA, but it is also helpful to have localized knowledge. You really need both to exploit the arbitrage. Not all locations will be profitable for STRs—that is an important point to note.

Q: *How much do you make off them monthly in high season? Low season?*

A: I try to engage in markets where there is consistent revenue year-round. I would say I make approximately two thousand to three thousand dollars in revenue per month per property, on average. So every four units is $100,000 in my pocket, not bad for the amount of work I do for them. Of course, I am in some markets that are more seasonally volatile. In Arizona, for example, I only break even in the low season, but profits are made in the winter, so you just have to stomach it for those three or four downturn months.

Q: *What are the three keys elements you need in a property to take advantage of this?*

A: 1) It needs to be in an advantageous location that is desirable to tourists and business travelers; 2) It needs to be in a regulatory environment that is favorable to STRs. There is no third element. If these two elements are met, then there is an opportunity for arbitrage at the property.

Q: *How long does it take for you to manage a property per week?*

A: It takes an average of three hours per property once a system is in place. However, when first obtaining the property and when exiting the property, the time commitment is much more, but that is a short-term commitment.

Q: *Please give your key tip or trick for hosting an Airbnb property.*

A: Be responsive and constantly alter pricing strategy.

Q: *What do you think of Airbnb's future with regulation?*

A: This is a very good question and not easily answered. This means the best answer is that it depends. It depends on the individual market, it depends on the economic climate of those markets, and it depends who is in power politically. It also depends macro-economically on who wins the war between hotels and Airbnb/VRBO. I believe some markets will be more STR-friendly than others, and investors will flock to those markets. For example, I would never invest in a STR in New York City; it wouldn't be profitable due to regulation. Same with London and Amsterdam. Their ninety-day restriction on STRs eliminates arbitrage profit opportunity. You *must* find markets that are sustainable.

Q: *Would you ever become part of the Experience program with Airbnb?*

A: Not personally, but I would love to find a way to partner with those that offer Experiences. I would also be a client.

Q: *What are the three most important qualities that can make someone become a Superhost?*

A: You must be responsive. You must be customer service-oriented; that includes going the extra mile by offering your guest little amenities like coffee and water. You must not cancel reservations; there is a zero tolerance for that.

Q: *What is the worst personal experience you ever had with a guest?*

A: I've been pretty lucky, no disaster stories. The worst is when a guest cancels because they are overly needy during the stay or when they are constantly messaging you about small irrelevant things. It takes up too much time and these guests can never truly be satisfied. But everyone is going to experience that; you just hope it's minimal, which it is.

Q: *How much money could one make taking advantage of long-term versus short-term rental if they did it full time?*

A: Haha, it really depends on how many properties one has. Going with my two thousand to three thousand dollars per property per month target I referenced, one can expect to make a significant amount correlated with the number of properties one hosts. I would say that four units is enough to quit your day job if you are not enjoying it, which most people hate their jobs.

Renting out Spare Bedroom to help pay Mortgage #1: Q & A with Laura Abbott

About Laura Abbott

Divorced mother of five, grandmother of two, real estate entrepreneur. I have renovated and flipped many houses, owned small apartment buildings and other single-family rentals. I have also hosted foreign exchange students from England, Amsterdam, China, France, Germany, Mexico, (and others) throughout the years. I love having people in my home, and I love cultural exchanges. Besides my Airbnb rentals, I am about to open two single-family Residential Assisted Living Homes here in Connecticut with the intention of opening eighteen more over the next three to five years. I will also be looking for more Airbnb rentals (working on one large project at present) because I love being able to offer homey atmospheres to visiting guests, often with fresh chocolate chip cookies.

Q: *How long have you been a host on Airbnb?*
A: One year.

Q: *Are you a Superhost?*

A: Not yet, but getting closer!

Q: *How many properties do you host currently?*

A: One property, two rooms. Working on a cottage on the same property.

Q: *How many properties do you currently have that you rent out a portion of the house?*

A: One.

Q: *What is your mortgage of your current house?*

A: Twenty-nine hundred dollars per month, 383,000-dollar balance.

Q: *How much do you make off them monthly in high season? Low season? Occupancy rate?*

A: Earned 1,250 dollars so far this month, which is high season in Connecticut. Low season is probably four hundred dollars a month, assuming seventy-five dollars a night.

Q: *What are the three key elements you need in a property to take advantage of this?*

A: Proximity to me, location, amenities.

Q: *How long does it take for you to manage a property per week?*

A: Twenty minutes per room in my home.

Q: *Please give your key tip or trick for hosting an Airbnb property.*

A: Keep the room/listing impeccably clean and offer extras. I bake cookies for my guests, am friendly, and communicative.

Q: *What do you think of Airbnb's future with regulation?*

A: Not sure. An attorney of mine is involved in regulating this at the state level in Connecticut. I told him to please interview me as someone who hosts. I want them to hear from more than the hotel lobby.

Q: *Would you ever become part of the Experience program with Airbnb?*

A: I have not evaluated this and am just learning about it.

Q: *What are the three most important qualities that can make someone become a Superhost?*

A: Cleanliness, quick/clear communication, and asking for excellent reviews.

Q: *What is the worst personal experience you ever had with a guest?*

A: I had some "needy" guests who booked one of my rooms, which clearly states that there are two twin beds in it, one of them being a trundle. Her less-than-stellar review stated that she peeked into another room (my daughter's room) and was upset that I didn't offer her the queen bed—even though my other Airbnb room, which was vacant, has a queen bed. She also complained that I didn't have milk, only non-dairy creamer, and felt that I was rushing them out in the morning because they had told me repeatedly that they were leaving early in the morning and I offered them to-go cups.

Q: *Are you an Airbnb guest as well?*

A: Absolutely!

Another Host Renting out Spare Bedroom to Pay Rent #3: Q & A with Tho

About Tho

Fun, friendly, and respectful family with two kids make your stay the most enjoyable and memorable. We love surfing, fishing, cycling, yoga and just enjoy the beach and the sunshine.

Q: *How long have you been a host on Airbnb?*

A: Since 2012, so it's about five years.

Q: *Are you a Superhost?*

A: No.

Q: *How many properties do you host currently?*

A: One property with three listings for three rooms in my five-bedroom home. I also occasionally list my timeshare week and once listed the hotel rooms I booked but couldn't use.

Q: *How many properties do you currently have on an arbitrage of long term versus short term?*

A: Two of the three rooms are on rent long-term after the short-term guests want to extend their stay. I prefer one room long-term and two rooms with short-term due to higher income but I can adjust that for the future.

Q: *How much do you make off them monthly in high season? Low season?*

A: Two thousand dollars per room on high season, one thousand dollars per room on low season.

Q: *What are the three key elements you need in a property to take advantage of this?*

A: Cleanliness, comfort, and welcoming atmosphere.

Q: *How long does it take for you to manage a property per week?*

A: Two to four hours.

Q: *Please give your key tip or trick for hosting an Airbnb property.*

A: Just do it—you will learn along the way.

Q: *What do you think of Airbnb's future with regulation?*

A: It's going to be more regulated and has more challenges than the hotel industry.

Q: *Would you ever become part of the Experience program with Airbnb?*

A: Yes.

Q: *What are the three most important qualities that can make someone become a Superhost?*

A: No cancellation, communications, and spotlessly managed property.

Q: *What is the worst personal experience you ever had with a guest?*

A: This woman booked two weeks and didn't turn up until day five. After staying for two days and disappearing again, she came back two days later and checked out the next day, calling Airbnb to get a full refund, which I don't agree with and is endorsed by Airbnb. She lied on the review and called me incessantly with foul words. She posted my phone number on dating and prostitute websites so I had men calling and texting me at all hours looking for sex. Worst of all, she called Child Protection Services, saying my husband and I did inappropriate things in front of our children during Thanksgiving dinner; we had other guests to instantly discredit and prove that it was an outright lie. My kids weren't even there because they went to bed at 7 p.m. Realizing she may be mental and dangerous, I finally hired an investigator and found out she had lots of criminal records and this is probably not the first time she did this to someone. Airbnb shut down her profile and I never heard from her again.

Q: *How much money could one make taking advantage of long-term versus short-term rental if they did it full time?*

A: The potential is unlimited.

Rented Their Luxurious Home to Pay for a Vacation: Q & A with David Baker

About David Baker

From a young age, David Baker has always believed that there is no limit to what a person can achieve if he puts his mind to it. After graduating from Point Loma Nazarene University in 1993, he was determined to pursue the highest paid profession at that time. Between investment banking and commercial real estate, he opted for commercial real estate. David started working for Flocke & Avoyer Commercial Real Estate leasing and selling retail shopping centers in San Diego. Though he quickly moved up to senior vice president, he knew in his heart that he was destined to invest and develop for himself.

In 2001, he founded Active Investments and started buying retail buildings in San Diego. He developed a knack for transforming unsightly properties into very attractive real estate, or as he describes it, "putting lipstick on a pig." Since 2001, he has amassed a portfolio of real estate that spans throughout San Diego County as well as Hawaii. In 2015, he created Barn Brewery in a building he owns in North Park, California, just outside San Diego. The small brewery has gone on to win various local accolades. In short, David now plays the real-life version of his favorite childhood game of Monopoly.

When he isn't working on his different holdings, chances are he is training for his next endurance challenge. Ultrarunning challenges such as Rim to Rim to Rim (fifty miles and twenty thousand feet of climbing in the Grand Canyon) and the TransRockies race in Colorado (a 120-mile running race in the Rocky Mountains at ten thousand feet elevation). He also enjoys surfing in Nicaragua, Hawaii, and Mexico, to name a few locations. David resides with his fiancée and his two beautiful kids in Coronado, where he is actively involved in his family, the community, and various charitable events.

Q: *How long have you been a host on Airbnb?*
A: One year.
Q: *Are you a Superhost?*
A: Not yet, but every guest has rated us five stars so far.
Q: *How many properties do you host currently?*
A: Two, my home in Coronado and a condo in Hawaii that is under my assistant's account, as she is a Superhost, because we rent out 100 percent when I am not visiting.
Q: *How much do you make off them monthly in high season? Low season?*
A: We get $1,450 per night year-round.
Q: *What is the minimum number of nights you will rent the property?*
A: Four nights minimum.
Q: *Do you view this income as paying the mortgage, or helping to pay for that European vacation?*
A: Helping to pay for worldwide travel.
Q: *What are the three key elements you need in a property to take advantage of this?*
A: Location and cleanliness. As long as it is clean and located in an area where people want to travel, then anyone can do it. Of course, design, model (stylish) furniture, a pool or Jacuzzi, game tables, bikes, paddle boards, TVs, movies, and the like, are all worth the investment too.
Q: *How long does it take for you to manage a property per week?*
A: No time at all. It really depends on how often you rent. We only rent about five to seven days each month, which gives us a great opportunity to travel. This requires little to no time managing. An hour to set up Airbnb, then responding to

an email. The largest job is the cleaning, which we hire out, so scheduling the crew to do that takes about five minutes. The most-asked question is how to set up the home for Airbnb. This process takes the most effort because you have to organize a system of locking closets, and the like. But once that is complete, it's easy. We leave pictures up. Food that will go bad, we throw out, but we leave food and spices in the pantry. I don't mind if the guests eat the food we leave, but most bring their own food.

Q: *Please give your key tip or trick for hosting an Airbnb property.*

A: I would invest in coded padlocks so guests don't have to deal with keys and definitely get a good housekeeper.

Q: *What do you think of Airbnb's future with regulation?*

A: I think everyone will have to pay the TOT or hospitality tax just like hotels, which is fine. I think some communities/smaller cities will ban them outright.

Q: *What is the worst personal experience you have ever had with a guest?*

A: I've never charged a guest a dime. Yes, we've had nice wine and cocktail glasses broken, a dirty house, and the like, but I figure if they are paying 1,450 dollars a night, I can eat one hundred dollars total "loss."

Interior Designer who works with Airbnb Hosts: Q & A with Vanessa Deleon

About Vanessa Deleon

Vanessa Deleon is a New York-based interior designer, product designer, blogger, brand ambassador, and lifestyle expert. Vanessa's innovative sensibility combined with a keen eye for details helps her clients' inspirations and ideas come to life. Vanessa's designs attract and inspire a long A-list clientele globally.

Vanessa has been featured in several coffee-table books and numerous publications. Her biggest accolades include the TV programs *Terry Crews Saves Christmas*, *American Dream Builders*, *Restaurant Impossible*, HGTV's *Generation Renovation*, *Designer Challenge*, *Bang For Your Buck*, *HGTV Design Star*, DIY's *Rev Run's Renovation*, *Ice Loves Coco*, and Bravo's *Million Dollar Listing*. She has made numerous guest appearances on *The Better Show* and NBC's *Today*, is contributing designer for Open House NYC and PIX 11's *Vanessa to the Rescue*, and was a host designer for YouTube's Channel Spaces TV *Your Place Is a Deal Breaker*. The International Foodservice Distributors Association (IFDA) and legendary Jamie Drake named Vanessa the Rising Star of Interior Design. She is the recipient of the Latina Trailblazer Award, Illustrious Awards, and Gold Coast Leadership Award. Vanessa has been named Editor at Large of the American Society of Interior Designers (ASID).

Q: *Are you currently an Airbnb host?*
A: No, I am not.
Q: *Have you ever used Airbnb as a guest?*
A: No, but many of my friends have been guests.
Q: *How many properties have you designed?*
A: Thousands, but six properties for Airbnb total to date.
Q: *What are the locations of these properties?*
A: Amsterdam, Miami, New York, and St. Martin.
Q: *Which unit is your favorite?*
A: St. Martin and Miami.
Q: *On a low-end budget, how much would it cost to furnish a one-bedroom?*
A: Two thousand dollars.

Q: *What are the three key elements you need in a property to take advantage of this?*

A: Wi-Fi, a comfortable bed, and great design.

Q: *How long does it take to turn a property from bare-boned to furnished and stunning?*

A: A couple of days, possibly one day if I have the manpower.

Q: *Please give your key tip or trick for designing an Airbnb property.*

A: A well-staged property, with pictures, will help rent the property. Do something that will stand out, such as a very cool swing chair hanging from the ceiling or a fun mural in the living space that represents the area. A daybed you can convert into a couch during the day and for sleeping at night is a great idea. Note that a daybed is the best furnishing to include in a dual-purpose room, totally versatile.

Q: *What are three most important qualities in maximizing a small square-footage unit?*

A: Try using items for dual purpose, such as a coffee table that serves as an ottoman or can be converted into a low eating table. Instead of a sofa, use a bed horizontally against the wall to create a sofa look, add some oversized pillows to rest against the wall, and now you have a very comfy sofa that instantly converts back into a bed. Hang up a bike rack on your wall foyer, as it doesn't take up floor space so your guest can have a place to hang a bike, or you can provide the bikes as a perk.

Q: *Do you have any Airbnb projects you are currently working on?*

A: I will soon—for a great new show I will be working on, hint hint, it might be with Andrew!

About AlphaShark.com

AlphaShark.com is an online trading room and classroom that allows its members access to live trading sessions during premarket, market, and post-market trading hours. The goal is to give people access to the valuable information they need to learn how to become effective traders and maximize their investments in the market.

Please note, Andrew is *not* an RIA and cannot give recommendations or advice, but he can offer his opinion and stocks and options as a day trade and swing trader.

Andrew, along with a team of expert traders, run the trading floor and are available to answer members' questions and give them insights into the trends they are noticing, and why. Also, webinars to continue growing and gaining knowledge in the ever-exciting, constantly changing world of trading are available.

The products available through AlphaShark.com include:

- Ten subscription-based models, one which includes the live trading room
- Educational courses on trading: to date, AlphaShark.com has sold over ten thousand educational courses that teach people how to trade
- Proprietary-based indicators: Alphashark.com has ten proprietary-based indicators that give traders

buy and sell signals based on technical analysis. These have become very popular and many of them have shown historical data for profitability and based on the Ichimoku Cloud.

For more details on all products and services visit:

www.AlphaShark.com/Products

Contact Information:

Andrew Keene
312-576-3210
Andrew@alphashark.com